The Third Talk
The Solution to Our Children's Greatest Challenge

by
John Van Arnam

The Third Talk®
2024

Editing services provided by Writerwerx University (GetBookHelp.com) and Cyndi Sandusky (SanduskyEditorial.com).

Cover design and book design by Tenesha L. Curtis (TeneshaLCurtis.com). Cover image by John Van Arnam.

Paperback ISBN: 979-8-3392-6644-0

Paperback version printed in the United States of America.

Table of Contents

INTRODUCTION

"We're engaged in the largest unsupervised experiment of young men in history, and it's porn. And the problem, beyond creating unreasonable expectations around what it means to be in a relationship with a woman, [is that] it quite frankly takes your mojo to get out of the house and meet someone and develop the skills to actually have your own sex—[porn] takes that away."

Scott Galloway
Professor, author, and speaker

My name is John Van Arnam. I am a man who is passionate about giving kids the very best chance to succeed that we can and then getting out of their way. Currently, I speak at schools, churches, community gatherings, and safety conferences, in living rooms and dining rooms, in kitchens, on porches, and at PTA events. I am a person of action and believe that "doing" beats "analysis" all day long. I have spent over two decades actively addressing the proliferation of youth exposure to internet pornography, and I feel we are at a place in America where we simply have to act. We as a nation must act. Underage American children are the largest viewing demographic of internet pornography in the world. Our kids see more porn than the entire country of Canada. Not Canadian children, the whole country. The same is true for England, Germany, France, India, Mexico, and Japan.

Writing this book for you is one of the ways I have decided to act. Never in the history of humankind has this much pornography, in such a medium, been so available to everyone at any age. Our children today are the unintended lab rats of an online social experiment. I am a dad. A man. A grown-up. I do not claim to have all the answers. I do claim to have this answer, and it is one that has been successful for a long time. The answer is to talk about it. And I have named this solution The Third Talk.

People are always curious about why I am so vehement about protecting children from this content, probing for the reason I'm so passionate. The truth is that I have discovered an ability to speak in front of parents and children together about avoiding internet pornography. I can do that in a way that does not shame, blame, or embarrass anyone. I can do that in a way that allows each participant, both kids and parents, to feel connected to one another and to be on the same page about a historically difficult conversation. Because I have an ability to do this, and it's so desperately needed right now, I believe I also have a responsibility to do it. That's it. That's my reason. I can do something to make the world better for our kids, so I should.

I also feel this message is too important not to socialize it in every way we can, everywhere we can. I sometimes feel that the folks who wonder why I am so passionate about this topic are also seeking a way that they can tune out this wildly uncomfortable subject and simply blame the messenger for the message. He is a conservative, a liberal, an atheist, a believer. He's blue, he's red, one of them, one of us, and so on. They seek a reason not to listen, because that is so much easier than actually having the conversation with kids or addressing the subject out loud in a meaningful way. It makes it much harder to tune me out when they find out that, for the most part, I'm normal(ish).

What people who are curious about my desire to help always seem to be expecting is some sort of political agenda or a religious ideology. But the simple truth is that I'm a grown-up who sees that our children are poisoning their brains with a behavior that we can help them avoid, and we're not doing that. To be perfectly candid, that ticks me off and drives my desire to act.

This book provides parents with the necessary tools they'll need to initiate a prevention-based conversation about pornography with their children. As the founder of The Third Talk, I'm going to delve into a few things you may never have heard before. Namely, how pornography directly causes mental, social, and even physical hurt to children who watch it—and even to those who don't watch it. I will discuss why parents don't talk about pornography and why they absolutely should. Throughout this book, I will use the terms "parent," "adult," or "grown-up" to refer to anyone who is caring for a child. This includes biological parents, but it also means grandparents, foster parents, court-appointed guardians, caregivers, and similar people.

You do not need to be a child's biological mother or father to be a child's "parent."

Throughout this book I will also use the words "porn" and "pornography." If that is uncomfortable for you, I encourage you to push through that discomfort for the sake of your child's health. I believe naming any problem is the first step to solving it. For years, and only for other people's comfort, I have used several other phrases like "explicit adult content," "inappropriate website material," and "hardcore online videos." But this is my book, and in it I am not going to dance around those words. Internet porn is the challenge that we, and our young people, face.

I'm going to provide you with an actual script that you can use to get this prevention conversation started between you and your kids. This includes the exact language to use, what you can expect your child's reaction to be, and what to do and say when things get awkward. I'll explain how to move past the embarrassment and how to do your best to save your children from the problems that come from their exposure to online pornography.

I placed the "script" part of the book up front. I expect that you may want to know how to have this conversation with your children right now, and you may not want to read through all the information on why exactly this method works. For those who are interested, those chapters come later in the book. I have included them so that you can get a better handle on how this is a cultural challenge, a mental health issue, a physical health issue, and potentially one of the most debilitating elements of being a young person growing up today.

I want to spur all caring adults to—for the sake of their children's long-term health—communicate openly about the dangers of watching porn. My goal is to encourage all parents to understand and acknowledge that internet porn is a huge problem for children and that parents are in the best position to keep our own children away from it. I am calling on parents to talk with their kids, talk with each other, and then collaborate with others in our communities. Especially those who have a direct hand in our children's daily lives, such as school administrators, state boards of education, pediatricians, guidance counselors, coaches, and lawmakers. I want us all to come together and take a united stand to make sure our children learn how to prevent exposure to porn or how to handle what they've already been exposed to. If we can do that, we could drastically reduce (and maybe even eliminate) the psychological and physical health problems that come from early exposure to porn.

I am thrilled to be able to provide you with the culmination of over two decades' worth of dedicated research, teaching experience, and family prevention meetings. This includes feedback from parents, teachers, principals, parent-teacher associations, students, law enforcement, and others who have successfully used The Third Talk method. I want to thank you and congratulate you on taking a positive step forward for your children's health and well-being.

You got this!

John Van Arnam
Founder, The Third Talk™

CHAPTER 1
The Other Talks

The First Talk:
The Birds and The Bees

I have called this strategy The Third Talk because it is one of multiple discussions most parents will have with their children. The first of these is generally referred to as "the talk" and deals with "the birds and the bees." This is a dialogue that, even today, parents can experience difficulty having with their children. It's the "sex" talk. This is an important conversation to have, as it will set the standard for what you and your family want and expect from your kids. Please do not abandon this talk. Please do not just have it once, get it over with, and never bring it back up. Your children are naturally curious, and they will explore their sexuality with or without your guidance. And this experimentation happens over the course of years, not a single conversation.

For example, some parents start having short talks about sex when their child is as young as three or four years old, making sure their children know the medical names of their body parts (penis, vagina, etc.). This talk can help young children understand that (1) no one is supposed to be touching them on their private parts (bathing suit area), and (2) they are to immediately tell a parent or trusted adult if someone does so. This helps prevent prolonged abuse and assists grown-ups with identifying pedophiles and bringing them to justice. Obviously, you want to provide your own input and guidance to your own children on this matter and many others. You don't want to leave this element of their lifelong and critical education up to anyone else. While it can be uncomfortable, parents need to have this talk as soon as possible.

The Second Talk: Sex Ed

The second talk happens somewhere around middle school, where a health teacher or guidance counselor will have a conversation with your child about anatomy, pregnancy, and sexually transmitted infections, usually in health class. They may have this talk in fifth grade, for about an hour, and then maybe again in eighth grade for an hour. And that's it. That's all they get. After that, our kids are left on their own to explore their own sexuality. Unfortunately for them, they'll do that online.

The Third Talk: Internet Pornography

We now need to have another conversation with our kids about truly healthy sexual socialization and why avoiding internet pornography is the most important first step. I have called this additional conversation The Third Talk. Internet porn acts as sex education for our children today, and that is just plain wrong. I am adamant that internet pornography cannot be a substitute for parental discussion regarding sexual education. I understand that this conversation is one that has been historically difficult for parents to have. But after reading this book, I promise you will be able to start the pornography prevention conversation with your kids.

Healthy Sex

Sex is different for everyone. And that's okay. We all have various preferences that we learn about and explore with our chosen sexual partners. Throughout this book I'll use words like "healthy" when referring to sex. I want to be clear here about what I mean when I say that, just to make sure we're all on the same page. Healthy sex is sex that is ethical, legal, and mutually pleasurable.

ETHICAL

Having sex ethically means doing things like pausing or stopping the encounter when the other party verbalizes or shows themself to be uncomfortable. This could mean pulling away, avoiding eye contact, or saying words like "no," "stop," or "don't." Ethical sex also means that if one person wants to try something new or different they tell their partner this and get clear consent (i.e., "Yes, let's try that.") before the new act begins. This might include changes such as new sexual positions or no longer using contraceptives. Forcing someone to have sex or to engage in specific sex acts that they are not comfortable with is not the basis for a healthy sexual or romantic relationship.

LEGAL

Having sex legally means only engaging in sex acts that are not deemed criminal. For example, two high schoolers may consent to having sex with one another. This would be considered consensual (ethical) sex. But if one is seventeen and the other is eighteen, the older child could be considered a sex offender in some states and circumstances. So while the act was ethical because both parties agreed, it wasn't legal. Engaging in illegal sex acts only creates risk and the potential for further harm for one or both parties.

MUTUALLY PLEASURABLE

Having sex that is mutually pleasurable means engaging in sex acts that both parties can enjoy until orgasm. For instance, let's pretend our example high school teens are both legal adults now. And they both want to have sex, having clearly agreed to do so with one another. If only one of them experiences anticipation, excitement, and ecstasy from the sexual activity (especially if this is a pattern over the course of multiple sexual encounters), it isn't mutually pleasurable intercourse. Over time, this can lead to a partner feeling neglected, confused, and hurt. If a sexual relationship is one-sided in this way, it can often cause relationship problems and even mental health issues for the partner who never or rarely finds the sex pleasurable.

Porn Doesn't Model Healthy Sex

I want children to grow up with a healthy idea of what sex is supposed to be. Not necessarily which specific acts a parent might consider good or bad (again, everyone is different). I want them to know that consent, the law, and pleasure are all important for them and their partners. I want them to know that they get to say who does what with their body (who can touch them, kiss them, etc.). I want them to be able to recognize when their boundaries are being violated by someone and know what to do about it.

Unfortunately, much of the pornography that children are being exposed to does not show these kinds of elements. Even though these are adult fantasies played out by paid actors, children don't necessarily understand this because no one has told them. We frequently discuss the unreal things that happen in movies because they are so over the top when compared to our reality. But if a child is secretly watching porn, they don't have anyone to have a conversation like that with. They may see people forced into sex acts even though they are actively communicating that they don't want to have sex. They may see people role-playing having sex with authority figures, such as stepparents or teachers or coaches. If they don't understand that this isn't healthy sex—that it's essentially just a skit that someone put on in order to earn some money and fame— then they can carry those scenes in their head as the model for what sex is supposed to be. And that is a major factor in causing the social and romantic problems that come from exposure to internet porn.

Moving Forward

Now you know how The Third Talk's topic is different from other chats about sex that your children may have engaged in with you or other adults in their lives. And you have a clear understanding of what I mean when I use the term "healthy" to refer to sex. In the next chapter, I'll show you the steps for having The Third Talk with your child. Though you will have multiple conversations about healthy sex and porn over the course of your child's life, my method will give you the information you need to start that series of exchanges with your child in order to help keep them safe from the painful impact that exposure to porn can have on them.

CHAPTER SUMMARY

• The "birds and the bees" talk about sex doesn't usually cover internet porn.

• The second talk that kids get in their health or science class at school also skips a discussion of porn.

• The Third Talk is a new, important addition to sexual education inside and outside the home.

• Without an explanation of what healthy sex is, kids may think that the porn they see is healthy.

• When kids' expectations of sex get warped by porn, they can experience physical, social, and romantic problems in their future relationships, and well-being.

CHAPTER 2
The Third Talk Solution

"The training was amazing, life changing to say the least. I was a little nervous after taking [John's] course on the way home about the talk I was going to have with my kids because I knew, after hearing him, I was going to have to have it. The Child Testimonials on his site and the things (he said) that seventeen-, eighteen-, and nineteen-year-olds said about, if they could go back, they wish they had someone that cared about them enough to have that conversation, it was a no-brainer. I knew it was going to have to happen. I got home, did it at dinner. Had the talk with my kids. And it was amazing how they opened up just by me asking the question. It's like they were waiting for someone to ask them that question and talk to them about it."

Officer Simmons
The Third Talk course attendee

CHAPTER OVERVIEW
- Shift your thinking about discussing porn with your children.
- How to start The Third Talk.
- Common reactions kids have to your first question.
- How to respond to your child's reaction.
- How to continue having conversations about porn exposure.

Adjust Your Thinking

Before you start The Third Talk with your child, it's important to understand what is likely going to happen once you do and to prepare your reaction. Going into the first interaction with the appropriate mindset helps encourage future communication and helps you avoid potential problems down the line. Keep in mind that the average age that a child sees porn for the first time is eleven. So in order to prevent them from regularly watching porn and arm them with techniques to help them stop porn exposure if someone else tries to show it to them, starting these talks is most effective at around eight or nine years old. If you will be having the talk with a child who is in their early or late teens, it can still be beneficial. Just be aware that they may have already been watching porn regularly and could have already started experiencing many of the psychological and physical problems that porn consumption can produce.

Keep It Casual

One of the worst things you can do with this conversation is turn it into some major family event. Scheduling a family meeting time to talk about it or taking your child to their favorite restaurant to discuss it are the kinds of things that make it even more awkward than it already might be. This can also have the negative effect of encouraging your kids to shut down, put up walls, or dismiss it altogether. Kids are amazing at waiting us out. Keeping it casual works because as parents, especially in the postmodern age, we want to prevent our children from experiencing any sort of discomfort whatsoever. This is where we as parents will jump in with some sort of justification for the conversation or the reasons we feel we need to have it. "It's just because I love you, honey . . ." can kill the conversation. Don't let that happen. There may be a little pain or discomfort when you bring up pornography with your kids for the first time, especially at the ages necessary to actually prevent the harm. It's okay. It only happens the first time. Don't count on a lengthy, in-depth, heart-to-heart conversation with your child the first time you bring this up. That would be great, and here's hoping that happens. But for their and your comfort, just keep the first interaction casual, light, and brief.

Save yourself and your child some time and trouble by starting the conversation at some point during the normal flow of your day in your home. This ensures that they are near a safe space, like their own bedroom, giving them an opportunity to retreat from the conversation if things get overwhelming for them. Trying to talk about this in the car on the way home from school—a place with no escape options— or at the mall with no privacy can cut the lines of communication off before you even get started. Keep things simple and casual and start the conversation at home in a very matter-of-fact sort of way.

As they open up the fridge after school to see what's in there, when they put their backpack down, while they're packing for a sleepover, before dinner in the kitchen, or after dinner before they head to bed for the night. These would all be good times to start The Third Talk.

Don't Show Judgement

The most difficult aspect for parents having The Third Talk is managing their reactions when they hear that their children have already watched pornography. Saying "I can't believe you watched that!" or "Are you kidding me?!" or "What will the neighbors think?!" is pretty bad. However, even a gasp or a sigh, clenching your jaw, biting your lip, shaking your head, or turning away can communicate the judgment you feel. Kids are perceptive. They pick up on this and can feel rejected and criticized without you having said a single word. Also, know that this is not their fault. They are trying to navigate the world they were born into, not one they created. If they've made missteps along the way (as we all have), that's just part of being human. But with The Third Talk we can help prevent further damage. Using short, non-blaming, open-ended questions, you can keep the lines of communication open between you and your child so that you can help keep them safe.

The point of these kinds of conversations is to be clear about what your opinions, values, and expectations are. This gives them a kind of mental guidebook for this aspect of their life that makes it easier to make healthy decisions. It also opens up the opportunity to be and remain a "trusted adult" in their lives. You do that by listening. Listening is "your part" of The Third Talk, parents, and it is critical to the successful outcomes we are all hoping for. Successfully manage the pornography prevention conversation, and you open up the ability to have the dating expectations conversation, assault prevention conversation, breakup conversation, risky behavior conversation, and many other important and potentially charged discussions that can be difficult to have within a family.

Getting Started

William of Occam conceived Occam's razor. This concept, put simply, states that the simplest solution is almost always the best. It's a problem-solving principle arguing that simplicity is better than complexity. And our solution to internet porn exposure for children is going to seem preposterously simplistic. I want to assure you that it took more than two decades to boil various experiences, research, and collaborations down to something this basic and easy to use. This included working with law enforcement, search engines, and governments, as well as communicating with a variety of parents, children, schools, and communities. All this is infused into two simple steps and five little words.

1. Ask your child: "Do your friends watch porn?"
2. Don't say another word until they respond.

Seriously, parents, not another word. If you can do that, you can protect your child from the harm of internet pornography. This is how you start that first and most important conversation about avoiding internet pornography. The silence can be excruciating, even if it only lasts a second or two while your kids are processing what just came out of your mouth.

As parents, we want to shield our kids from pain and discomfort. It can be so hard that we feel like we just have to jump in and say something. Parents usually want to jump in with a phrase like "I just love you so much, honey," or "I'm worried about you, and I just want you to know . . .," just to hear something other than awkward silence.

Instead, during The Third Talk, sit with your child in that awkwardness. Give them the time to feel it fully. They are now just as uncomfortable as you were when you were planning to have this conversation after reading this book. Maybe even more so. When they woke up that day, they likely never imagined this conversation was going to come up. Let them recover from the surprise and answer you. You would die for your children. Give up every dime you have and forgo sleep and food if it meant that you could keep them safe. That's a beautiful thing. That willingness to suffer for them is part of what being a parent is all about. Your willingness to endure terrible pain for them comes from the natural instincts of being a parent and having experienced your own discomfort in your life. But going against that tendency in this moment is what is going to save your child. You're trading a temporary discomfort for them to have a healthier, happier life in the decades to come. This is what you are giving your child, and they deserve it. Do not take that away from them.

This moment you will find yourself in reminds me of taking my own children to get their shots as babies. They were infants, completely in my charge. They received the first shot in their arm, looked at me, and began to cry. The look on their face seemed to ask why I would let this strange person hurt them. I'm Dad. How could I betray them so badly and stand there while they were hurt? Why? The answer is because I knew it was good for them. I knew they would be better off in the long run to have experienced that instant of a little pain. They didn't think so, of course. They just thought the doctor was bad. I was there to protect them from bad people, and I wasn't doing it. Their looking up at me with giant tears forming in their eyes, pleading with me to take away this pain, did not dissuade me from helping them, caring for them, knowing what was good for them, and allowing that pain. And then, after the pain, fear, and anguish began to subside for them a little bit, up comes that second shot.

In that context, allowing my children to feel fear, pain, anger, and disbelief didn't make me a bad dad. Not allowing that temporary pain for the sake of their long-term health would've made me a bad dad. So if you're willing to do that to keep them safe, staying quiet for a few moments while they absorb what they just heard from you isn't quite as drastic by comparison, right? You can do this, parents.

Internet porn is a brain-altering physiological and psychological hurt that, unless you're as lucky as a lottery jackpot winner, your kids will experience. Porn will present challenges that may affect your child for the rest of their life in ways that you, and they, do not yet fully understand. Statistically, your kids start watching porn at age twelve and will see tens of thousands of videos before they leave high school. Sorry if that is hard to read, parents. It's just the truth, whether we like it or not.

If saber-toothed tigers were still walking the earth, we'd be pretty adamant about steering our children clear of them. Remember polio? We stayed on that one until we got it right. Mumps, measles, AIDS, COVID, take your pick. We did not conquer those challenges by shrinking away from them, making light of them, or hoping that they would go away. We saw the problem, agreed it was a problem, and did something about it.

After you ask "Do your friends watch porn?" your child will likely have one of a few reactions. Let's take a look at them and some ways for you to respond.

They'll Say "Yes"

Be prepared for this answer. In my work, this is always the biggest surprise for parents short of walking in on their child in the act of watching porn. "Yes" can be a showstopper for parents, and ironically or not, this is an answer that a lot of parents get. Be ready. Be prepared with your best "poker face." Be primed to hold a calm facial expression and not display disbelief, anger, surprise, sadness, or shame. Practice your non-reaction in the mirror in the days leading up to having The Third Talk. Your initial reaction will influence all future conversations you have with your child about this issue.

If your child says "yes" to this question from you, it's a safe bet that they have been watching porn as well. As painful as it might be to know, statistically it makes sense. After all, they have the internet in their pockets and backpacks all day long through smartphones and tablets. If they admit that their friends watch porn, now is not the time to put them in the hot seat about it. This kind of interaction with you is too new. Asking a follow-up question like "How do you feel about that?" or "What do you think about that?" or even "Why do you think they watch it?" can keep the conversation going without getting into unnecessary details or making them feel judged about what their friends (or they) are doing. "I didn't know that" is my favorite response to any statement your child makes about porn. "I didn't know that" is honest, it makes them the expert, and it keeps them talking to you, which is the whole point!

You are not trying to "solve" this in one quick conversation; please remember that. This will take time and your continual participation and communication. Allowing them to dominate the conversation and to walk away whenever they want to is key here. Walking away feeling unjudged, unpunished, or even uncomfortable with the conversation means the next conversation will be easier. The longer you stand there listening to them, the more trust is being created, and the more healing and protection happens.

An ideal situation is that you ask the first question and your child talks themself out of watching porn on their own while you nod, listen, and occasionally add your own input. And that's not pie-in-the-sky wishful thinking; I have personally watched this happen.

You're not the expert here. Your children are. Only they know what it's like to grow up and go through puberty and adolescence with internet porn at their fingertips literally every second of the day. Only they know what it's like to have to manage their own sexuality within the background of internet pornography in our postmodern times. Yes, you were their age at one point. But the technology, social environment, and circumstances were all wildly different. Accept that you must rely on them to educate you on what's going on with people their age right now. Not ten, twenty, or forty years ago. Your experience isn't what's important at this moment. What your children are going through right now, that is important. You need to protect your children from the world they live in, not the world you wish they lived in, and listening to their experience on this topic is the very best way to start.

They'll Splutter

Your child may be so startled by your question that they spit out a series of "ugh," "um," "sheeh," "wha," "mo," "phew," "shh," and "ahh" sounds that young people make when they're caught off guard. When things get weird, this is a common response from young people. The spluttering and trying to find the words to express their extreme discomfort, the fidgeting and twisting of their facial features and limbs, the huffing and sighing—all of it is par for the course in uncomfortable situations. As I stated earlier, they did not know this question was coming, so they may need to mentally regroup in order to begin to seriously start talking about it with you. This sputtering may be exactly how they do it, and that's okay. Let them show their shock and embarrassment. Remember not to jump in verbally to save them. Allow them to hem and haw and gush and sputter. Just wait for them to recover and respond to the question.

They'll Say "No"

This response is unlikely, though not statistically impossible. Having twenty-four-hour access to a device that can take them to any porn site on the internet makes even just stumbling upon pornographic content nearly guaranteed. So not a single one of their friends watching porn would be pretty rare. Internet porn is simply too common and pervasive. In the vast majority of cases, children are in consistent contact with at least one friend (if not many or all) who have seen porn or who watch it regularly. This depends a lot on your child's age and who their friends are.

America watches 40 percent of the world's porn. Our children watch a little over a third of that. That works out to a very conservative 531 porn videos viewed by our underage American children every second of every day, 365 days a year. I'll save you the math: that's almost seventeen billion explicit adult videos viewed by underage American children every year. Obviously, the older they get the more they watch. Again, that is a very conservative number, easily defended, and I did that on purpose. Those numbers are also from before the COVID pandemic when viewership spiked while kids were home learning virtually. If we used our most aggressive numbers, it is almost twice that many. The odds are that your child is lying to you if they say that their friends don't watch porn. This is just another way to sidestep the conversation because it's uncomfortable. Now is not the time to call them on it or to try to get them to "confess" that their friends watch porn. Remember to keep using short, nonjudgmental, open-ended questions to keep them engaged in the conversation with you. An example in this scenario might be, "Do your friends know any kids who watch porn?" to take the spotlight another step away from your child and their social circle. You could also ask, "What do you think about them not watching porn?" and then give them time and space to answer you.

They'll Run

Understand that your child may "flee" when you ask them the question "Do your friends watch porn?" They could retreat to their room, a friend's house, or any part of the house where you are not present to put some distance between themself and this odd exchange they just had with you. That's okay too. Let them go. More opportunities to discuss this further will arise. You don't need to trap them and start interrogating them like a cop. Remember, if they walk away after you've asked them "Do your friends watch porn?" you haven't "lost" them. It isn't over, and you haven't failed. It is a sign of trust and respect that you do not follow them down the hallway and try to verbally "justify" why what you asked them is so important. It's important because you said it's important. You don't have to prove anything. You may have waited years to have this talk with your children. Most parents that I speak with have. Waiting another day or two is not going to change where they are. Give them time, space, and respect. You can then broach the subject again, calmly. Just don't give up on it. The rewards will be life changing for your children and for you.

They'll Ask "Why?"

One of the less common responses to the question "Do your friends watch porn?" is "Why?" They may want to know what prompted you to ask this question "out of the blue," which is fair. You may have been planning this for days or weeks, but they knew nothing about it.

The simplest way to deal with this question is to pull the conversation back around to your original question as you answer. It helps to be respectful by giving them an honest answer, but you also want to hold your ground on asking the question about their friends and porn. Remember not to get into your worries and concerns at this point ("I'm worried you're watching porn," "I'm concerned your friends may be showing you porn," etc.). Focus on facts and statistics and then get the conversation back on track. Here are some examples:

• "I heard some surprising things about how often kids watch porn online. Do your friends watch porn?"

• "I read that Billie Eilish had some traumatic experiences watching porn when she was eleven years old, and I wondered if anyone you knew might be going through something like that. Do your friends watch porn?"

• "I just finished a book about porn and realized that I never bothered to ask you about it. Do your friends watch porn?"

• "I heard that porn fires all the same receptors in the brain as heroin, methamphetamine, and cocaine. Do your friends watch porn?"

• "I heard that American children see over 531 porn videos every second of every day. Do your friends watch porn?"

• "In 2017, Net Nanny said that searches for pornography go up 4,700 percent in the hours after school lets out. Do your friends watch porn?"

No judgment, criticism, blame, embarrassment, or contempt. Just be a curious, concerned parent asking a straightforward question about your child's life, and then listen to the answer. It has been my experience that children want to talk about this. Maybe because I'm not their parent, it's easier for kids to speak with me, but I have never had to convince a child to tell me about their porn habit. On the contrary, they talk about it all openly. They are curious (sometimes scared), and that is where healing starts. If you speak and listen without judgment, parents, they will talk with you about this over and over.

They'll Ask If you Watch Porn

While this won't often be the immediate response, it can come up in this initial conversation or others that you have down the road. As always, the best policy is open and honest communication. If you haven't seen pornography before, fine. Truthfully tell them that you haven't. If you ask "Do your friends watch porn?" and their first response happens to be "Do you?" give your honest answer and then get right back to the question at hand. For example, "Yeah, I've seen it before as an adult. Do your friends watch porn?" or "Internet porn wasn't a thing when I was your age, so I never ended up thinking to look at it. Do your friends watch porn?"

The focus of this conversation isn't about you as a parent, it's about them as children. The key issue being that, even if you decided to watch an hour of porn every week, you are doing it as an adult who (1) is legally allowed to do so, (2) has the understanding that these are actors playing roles and that sex in real life commonly does not look like the sex portrayed in porn, and (3) your brain has developed enough that you can more easily manage any spikes in dopamine that watching porn may provide without becoming addicted.

Consider an analogy of drinking alcohol. If you got home after work, grabbed a beer from the fridge, sat on your couch, and drank that beer, you're not breaking any rules or laws. If your twelve-year-old came home after you and grabbed a beer and sat down on the couch next to you, you would probably have something to say. That does not make you a hypocrite regarding drinking alcohol. Just like with watching porn, drinking a can of beer one night is something you are legally sanctioned to do, that your body is mature enough to handle without damage, and that you are self-aware enough (hopefully) to manage so that you don't drink until you get drunk.

So as a parent, even if you have watched, or still watch, pornography, it's not hypocritical for you to have this discussion with your child. It's reasonable and rational for you to not want them to watch it. In later talks about their exposure to porn, feel free to openly share with them the reasons why adults watching porn and kids watching porn are two vastly different situations. In the later sections of this book, I provide plenty of statistics and recommended reading to increase your knowledge about porn's impact on developing brains. But for now, if this happens to be their initial reaction to your question, just give a short, honest answer and repeat "Do your friends watch porn?"

After the First Question

Once you've gone through the first experience of asking "Do your friends watch porn?" you've gotten through the worst of it. For years, parents have told us that all of the awkwardness is over after the words "Do your friends watch porn?" first come out of their mouth. The topic is on the table, and the path to further communication about it has been set. Getting through asking this initial question and listening to the answer makes later conversations much more comfortable and smoother.

Once the dialogue has been initiated, it is up to you to keep the conversation going over time, all the way through adolescence and on into their teens and adulthood. You can do that by going back to the original question and then just listening. Parents usually find that once the conversation is initiated and continued it becomes much like the other "talks" they've already been having about things like dating or smoking.

You want to eventually interject that you do not approve of your child watching pornography. But please wait and establish trust first, before you create rules or consequences related to porn viewing. Here are a few other open-ended questions you could use to initiate a pornography prevention conversation with your kids. After the first question, these could also be used in the following days, weeks, and months to help you continue conversations about online pornography with your kids.

● "Have you ever seen porn [on a school bus/at a party/at school/at a sleepover]?"

● "Do you know what a 'waist-up' is?"

● "Has anyone ever sent you a nude picture?"

● "Can people download porn on a video game console like a PlayStation or Xbox?"

● "Can people download porn on a phone?" (I really like the idea of using this question when you're standing in the kitchen or sitting in the living room with your phone in your hand!)

● "Have you heard of PIED (pornography-induced erectile dysfunction)?"

● "Have you heard of arousal deficiency (the female equivalent of PIED)?"

● "How do you feel about me asking you all these questions about porn?"

● "If you were going to protect your little brother/sister/cousin from porn, what would you say to them?"

Asking any of these simple questions can start your follow-up conversations about porn. Listening is the key to effective communication here, and you do not need to be, or even appear to be, "right" on this topic. Be fully, realistically, actually available to your child, even if this means not saying a thing. I have led this conversation for years, in situations where the whole family is present, and just listening seems to be the hardest part for parents, and the most important. Another difficult aspect of this interaction that can be hard for parents to come to terms with is openly admitting to gaps in their knowledge. But this is key to clear and healthy communication. There's no need to get defensive or try to make up answers you don't have. Just admit you don't know, keep asking questions, and keep quiet while your child speaks (and educates you!). Listening and saying "I don't know" can be powerful.

Talk Lapses

Though you may understand intellectually the importance of having multiple conversations about online pornography, you may have trouble coming back to the conversation regularly. While you don't need to discuss it every day, or even every week, asking a question related to online pornography multiple times per year or even once a month can keep the communication flowing between you and your child. You don't want to overwhelm yourself or your child by constantly asking about it. At the same time, you don't want so much time to pass without talking about it that the next time you bring it up it's almost as uncomfortable as the first time.

As a parent, you're busy. On top of raising your children and spending time with your spouse or dating partner, you have a job that you have to perform well at each week, you have bills that you have to pay, you have friends who reach out to you for support, you have extended family that you want to spend time with and care for, and you have your own self-care tasks that you need to complete for your own mental and physical health. Therefore, as important as these talks are, it makes sense that they can slip your mind sometimes. Don't be afraid to schedule reminders for yourself, if that's going to help you touch base with your kids about online pornography and keep your conversations going. Make sure the reminder is placed somewhere that is easily visible so you will see it multiple times each week, so you won't forget it as easily. Some examples might include:

● A note in your personal weekly planner once every two or three weeks.

● An event on your phone's digital calendar that will alert you when it's time to ask about it again.

● A small symbol on the family calendar in the kitchen that only you understand. Something innocuous, like a blue dot or a red check mark.

● Be sure to have random short conversations, such as when the cousins are coming over or if your child is going on a sleepover or an overnight field trip with a scout troop.

Then, whenever it's time to ask about their pornography experiences again, do it as soon as you notice it's the week or day that you've put on your calendar. Just like with the first time you brought it up, be sure to ask about it in a safe space and to ask short questions and listen.

Protecting Your Child with The Third Talk

Knowing how to have The Third Talk puts you in a great place to begin protecting your child from porn exposure. By starting a simple conversation, you can unlock a new level of open, honest, clear communication with your children about everything from internet porn to curfew. If you're interested in what makes The Third Talk so effective, I'll explain that in the next chapter.

CHAPTER SUMMARY

● Adjust your thinking to be ready to have The Third Talk with your child.

● The Third Talk is not a time to blame, judge, or punish your child for whatever they tell you.

● Practice or role-play with a trusted adult so that you will be ready to hear answers you won't like without reacting.

• Don't make a big "to-do" about this conversation. Have it during the normal course of their daily activities.

• Ask "Do your friends watch porn?" and say nothing else until they respond.

• Keep it casual. This is a simple question asked out of curiosity, not for the sake of blaming, judging, or punishing.

• Most kids actually want to talk about porn, so be someone who listens.

• "I don't know, that's why I'm asking" is an appropriate answer to almost any question.

• In order to prevent children from being caught off guard when they're exposed to pornography, conversations about it need to begin at around age eight and should continue throughout their teen years.

CHAPTER 3
The How

"I got my first iPod Touch when I was eight and a half years old. My parents thought they were doing everything right. And looking back, I severely regret that purchase, because by the age of nine I became fully addicted to pornography."

"MJ"
Attended The Third Talk at the age of eighteen. Full interview available at TheThirdTalk.org.

CHAPTER OVERVIEW

• The Third Talk expresses a lot more than just your curiosity.

• Starting this conversation increases trust in your relationship with your child.

• The Third Talk can be a healing force for kids who have been watching porn regularly.

Now for those of you who want to know more about how The Third Talk works and why the methods outlined in the previous chapter are so important, the remaining sections of this book will lay all that information out for you. While you can certainly execute The Third Talk with everything included in the earlier portions of the book, this information provides you with background on the science, theories, and statistics related to why The Third Talk is so effective. This knowledge may improve your ability to facilitate The Third Talk with your children.

The Power of Five Words

How is it possible that these five words can hold so much power? Keeping your child from a lifetime of hurt seems like a pretty big undertaking, and it should be more complicated. It's the ongoing conversations that save your children. But those five words are wildly powerful. They can start the adolescence-long conversation. You cannot ask this once and then consider it "handled." You need to continue talking to your children the same way you would about drinking, vaping, and riding in cars. Refraining from watching internet porn is a major challenge. It's a new world, and we need a new strategy for dealing with this threat to our children's health and well-being.

"Do your friends watch porn?" is a question that does several things at the same time. Used exactly as described (meaning ask those five words and don't say anything else), you open up a dialogue with your child on this sensitive topic. You also do several other beneficial things you may not even realize.

They Know That You Know

No beating around the bush. When you ask your child "Do your friends watch porn?" they now know that you know that internet pornography exists. This may be a brand new fact for them. Also, when you come right out and ask about it, you get the most uncomfortable part of the process over with as quickly as possible. The subject has been broached! You are now open to talking about it and listening to them talk about it. I equate this to jumping into a cold lake. It's easier if you just jump in. You know you'll get used to the water in about ten seconds, but you'll have to get through that initial discomfort.

You Focus on Other People in a General Way

Asking if "you" watch porn feels wildly different from asking if "your friends" watch porn. Asking "do you watch porn?" or "Does [insert a friend's name] watch porn?" will bring up walls. It's too intimate a question to ask out of nowhere, and your child will likely do one of two things: clam up or lie. If they clam up, they'll be adamant about remaining silent to avoid both lying to you and telling you that they or the friend you asked about watch porn. If they lie, they'll probably feel guilty about it, which can turn into resentment toward you for even asking them and putting them between a rock and a hard place. This is why the question is formulated to take some of the pressure off you and your child while still tackling this tough conversation. After all, you don't need the specifics (including information about any particular friend) since you aren't going to be punishing, blaming, or judging.

Asking about their friends in a general way invites them to respond. Kids get lectures all day long from adults. Saying things "at" them is a solid way for what comes out of your mouth to bleed into the background noise of their lives. But when you ask a question instead of making a statement, you change the pattern of what they're used to hearing from grown-ups. This makes them more open to paying attention. The question is also an opportunity for them to engage in a conversation with their parent about something they may have been hiding for a long time. Getting a chance to have a real conversation about a topic instead of having to sit and quietly listen to you, or anyone else, drone on about it is often a welcome change of pace for your child. This makes it easier for them to be engaged and open with you about the subject. Let them teach you about what they know about porn. Being an inquisitive seeker of knowledge in this moment, and not a disciplinarian, will work wonders.

It Respects Them as Experts of Their Own Experience

Parents cannot authentically be knowledgeable about what it's like to grow up with the current social climate, societal norms, and technological advances that kids encounter every single day. You don't know. You are not going through adolescence right now. Asking your child to teach you about it highlights and respects the fact that their individual experience is unique and even their general experience is vastly different from your own. Allowing them to tell you what it's like could convince them to do all the talking. That is what we are striving for, parents. Your kids telling you all about it while you listen without judgment. I wish that for all of you! Every grown-up reading this book. That is my hope for you and your family. Remember, parents, it is how you approach this conversation that will determine its outcome, and by default, your child's long-term health. One of the most unexpected elements for parents when having The Third Talk is their own sense of relief. Most parents have said to us that they did not expect that. It's just a bonus they get while trying to keep their kids safe. After helping your young children avoid a significant exposure and hurt, you may feel better as well.

Giving your child space and time to express their experience will help you gain knowledge and understanding of what the world is like from their perspective. After you start The Third Talk by asking that first question, you'll learn about elements of your child's world that you may not have known about previously. Use this information to continue the conversation about exposure to porn. It can make your child feel heard and increase the chances that they'll have additional and even more meaningful conversations with you next week and next month and next year.

It's a Grassroots Effort

Grassroots, parent-led initiatives are historically the most effective way to change culture for kids. If you think about Mothers Against Drunk Driving (MADD) or any of the other grassroots efforts made by parents to protect children from various dangers (cigarettes, alcohol, not wearing seat belts, etc.), this type of groundswell is effective. When I was growing up, bike helmets were just for wimps. Then we realized we spent $5.8 billion per year on brain injuries from childhood bike accidents. So the nation came together through community discussions, television ads, billboards, and school initiatives to make sure that kids wore helmets while riding their bikes. The Third Talk is a similar kind of intervention. It's a metaphorical bike helmet for your child, specifically designed to protect them from the harm of internet porn. And if we can get parents throughout the world to understand the importance of this "helmet" (The Third Talk) to protect against internet pornography exposure, we can save a lot of lives.

It's a Low-Cost Solution

The Third Talk is the least expensive way to change culture for our children. We should have a government-funded, moon-shot type of effort in place to keep our kids from watching porn nationally. But we don't. The US government should be spending billions of dollars a year on awareness, public service announcements, billboards, and nationwide education to help keep kids from watching porn and to understand the myriad ways this content can cause harm to their developing brains and bodies. But they don't. We should teach avoiding exposure to internet porn in every public school health class across the nation repeatedly, year after year. But we don't.

Unfortunately, to prevent pornography exposure, we'd need to start in about fourth grade, and that is just too problematic for almost all parents and school administrators to wrap their heads around. So instead we just . . . don't. The least expensive way to protect your children from the hurt of internet pornography is for you to discuss this topic with your own kids. The cheapest way to accomplish this tremendous task is by word of mouth. Parent to parent, family to family, community to community.

How The Third Talk Heals

In the hundreds of homes where I have met with families for coaching sessions, I've never witnessed the children in those families sitting with their hands folded staring at the floor waiting for the conversation to end. Ever.

From time to time the conversation starts off quiet or slow. But without fail, and very early on, when kids hear their grown-ups talking about pornography without judgment, embarrassment, shame, or blame, the kids light up. They begin to shed their guilt and fear about this topic. They start sharing their experience, now that there is a safe space in which they can do so. It can come out of their mouths like water from a fire hydrant. One of the most rewarding elements of the work I do is to watch the guilt, shame, and fear come streaming out of their mouths, off their chests, and away from their hearts. It is truly rewarding, my favorite part of the work, and I am grateful for it.

I have seen children who alleviate themselves of pent-up guilt, fear, and shame that they have been carrying around with them without their parents knowing—sometimes for years—simply by a grown-up initiating this topic. Kids are not going to bring this up to you because it's so uncomfortable for them to do so. But they also may feel as if their parent would never be willing to listen to them without judgment or blame. Remember, parents, it is not your child's fault that porn exists. It is not your child's fault that cell phones exist. It is not your child's fault that human beings are hardwired to be curious about other human beings without their clothes on. It is not your child's fault that porn has followed (or led) just about every technological breakthrough humans have accomplished for thousands of years. It is not your child's fault that cell phones, internet pornography, and normal, natural, healthy human curiosity and desire have created a perfect storm that causes this content to be easily available and overwhelmingly compelling. They are the victims of this perfect storm, and we have to treat them that way and never blame them for the conditions outside.

Imagine that your child was fishing on a boat in the ocean and a "perfect storm" came out of nowhere. A storm that no one saw or could have predicted or planned for. Imagine that storm capsized their boat and left your child to toss and turn in the ocean trying to tread water for weeks, months, or even years (or however long it has been since you have spoken with them about porn). They finally get washed up on a beach somewhere, tired, scared, hurt, and hungry. Then imagine, after they come to and gather their senses, you rush to their side. But instead of inquiring about their possible injuries or holding them and assuring them everything will be all right, you yell at your child and blame them for the weather conditions, wind direction, rudder position, weight distribution, bait choice, etc. How would saying things like "You should never have gone out to sea fishing in the first place!" or "You're grounded and can never go fishing again!" help heal their battered bodies and ease their fears? The answer is, it wouldn't. And reacting to them like this in regard to trying to navigate the world as a young person with access to porn also would not be helpful. Instead, we should be helping, empathizing, listening, and supporting them.

Our children need more parents and caring adults who will sit that shipwrecked kid down, wrap a blanket around them, and tell them they're safe and loved and cared for. We need adults to fix the boat, check the weather report, and then send that child back out to sea with the proper maps, information, supplies, and communication tools. We need to be the adults who will guide them and teach them so they can get through any terrible situation and become great skippers who are ready to explore the world safely. The Third Talk helps you be that loving person who will care, listen, and provide guidance instead of yelling, punishing, or criticizing.

CHAPTER SUMMARY

● The Third Talk was specifically crafted to ensure that you can have a safe, open conversation with your kids about porn.

● Talking about porn exposure is an ongoing thing, not a "one and done" discussion.

● Having The Third Talk shows your child that you are an adult who will listen.

● This simple interaction with children can be an effective, low-cost solution to porn exposure and management that strengthens your family and your community.

CHAPTER 4
The Problems

"I used to watch a lot of porn, to be honest. I started watching porn when I was like eleven. I thought that's how you learned how to have sex. I was watching abusive porn, to be honest. You know, when I was like fourteen. And I, you know, thought I was one of the guys and would talk about it and think I was really cool for not having a problem with it and not seeing why it was bad. I think it really destroyed my brain. And I feel incredibly devastated that I was exposed to so much porn. I think I had sleep paralysis and these, like, almost night terrors/just nightmares because of it. I think that's how they started because I would just watch abusive BDSM. I couldn't watch anything else, like, unless it was violent. I didn't think it was attractive. And I was a virgin. I had never done anything. It led to problems where the first few times I had sex I was not saying no to things that were not good. And it's because I thought that that's what I was supposed to be attracted to."

Billie Eilish
Singer and songwriter
"The Howard Stern Show" (December 2021)

CHAPTER OVERVIEW

- The internet has changed the world as we know it.
- Viewing porn is a global crisis for children.
- Tech-savvy kids are well equipped to get around content filters.
- The environment our children are growing up in is nothing like our upbringing.
- Watching pornography increases the likelihood of several negative consequences.

I've noted in general terms that watching internet porn can be both physically and mentally harmful. In this chapter, I'll dive a bit deeper into how porn contributes to various negative outcomes and how those negative outcomes impact families, communities, and nations.

Health Problems

The internet has changed the modern world in countless ways. Unfortunately, not all of those changes were for the better. Younger generations are native to this new digital world and are able to navigate it effortlessly. But this ease of access can lead to viewing inappropriate content. This exposure is dangerous for the physical development of their brains, their mental health, and their futures as happy, functional members of society. It can also simply take all the fun out of being young and exploring the wonderful natural elements of their individual sexuality. Internet pornography increases the chances that your child will experience one or more dangerous outcomes. I've listed some of them below, just to give you a basic idea of how internet porn (something kids have fast, easy, open access to) can impact your child's mental and physical health.

Brain Damage

So many good people have spent much of their careers outlining, in peer-reviewed papers and books, the effects of porn on a child's brain. I encourage you to visit the links at the end of this book to review some of those studies. At the end of the day, the most important thing for you to understand is that online pornography can have devastating, lifelong consequences for your children.

I'll paraphrase some of those studies for you by saying that porn can alter the structure and development of a child's brain. Studies show that porn can damage a developing prefrontal cortex. This area of the brain is critical for decision-making and impulse control. When the prefrontal cortex is damaged, children are more likely to act impulsively and make poor decisions. Porn is changing your child's brain. I have seen children go through years of expensive therapy in order to reverse this damage. Imagine taking your twelve-year-old to see a therapist once or twice a week for the symptoms of porn addiction. Imagine the embarrassment and shame your child might feel every time you take them to that office. Imagine the stress that situation could put on your relationship with the other caring adults in your kid's life. Imagine the financial toll that each of those sessions would take on your family. Imagine the days and weeks of time lost throughout the year when your child could be engaging in extracurricular activities, spending time with friends, or just hanging out with family. All of this could be the result of you simply not having The Third Talk with your child. This is why I think having this talk is so critical for your family.

In 2020, the British Board of Film Classification (BBFC) published a report indicating that 56 percent of kids ages eleven to thirteen interviewed said they should have been prevented from watching pornography by their parents. They cited ". . . because it messed up my brain . . ." as the most common response. I conducted a study of a group of eighteen-year-old college freshmen who, despite a high desire for independence, still wanted guidance from trusted adults on this topic and others. Every student interviewed craved structure, advice, and thoughtful education. They explained that they would have listened to their parents had they said "don't watch pornography." But their parents never spoke to them about porn at all, and they did view pornography, and each ended up with a host of problems that could easily have been avoided by parental interference. The video "Wake Up, Parents" is available to watch on TheThirdTalk. org, and it is heartbreaking.

On December 13, 2021, internationally famous pop star Billie Eilish appeared on The Howard Stern Show and uttered, "Porn messed up my brain." Her words dropped like a bomb as she went on to describe the mental and physical effects watching pornography had on her life since she became addicted to it at age eleven. Eilish, an adult at the time of the interview, didn't understand what she was watching as a little girl. How could she? The violent, degrading, and unrealistic images that are par for the course in online porn wouldn't register with most preteen brains as anything other than "real world" depictions of sex.

Billie Eilish's story is so typical, but most parents can't absorb it. Her candor surrounding this topic reminded me of the "Magic Johnson moment" regarding HIV. In 1991, the Los Angeles Laker MVP, twelve-time All Star, and nine-time member of the All-NBA First Team, announced that he was HIV positive. Until that point, many people associated HIV with anal sex and drug addiction and thought of it purely as a disease afflicting homosexual men and intravenous drug users.

Magic Johnson became a great equalizer. He demonstrated that HIV could be contracted by anyone, and it was okay to talk about it. He shifted the public conversation about HIV away from the topic of morality and instead into the area of public health. Johnson's candor changed the way the world viewed the HIV epidemic and made us realize that anyone, even a world-famous basketball star, could contract it. As a result, people began practicing safer sex, talking about it with their partners, and getting tested for STDs more frequently. HIV (and therefore AIDS) became less of a threat because we were more cognizant of it and started talking about it openly. Talking about porn the same way can have a similar impact on the world, especially when using The Third Talk as a framework.

Psychological Distress

In the same BBFC studies mentioned above, teenage girls were asked why they watched porn. In 2016, the answer was "because we want to know what our boyfriends want." In 2020, the number one answer changed to "to protect ourselves from PTSD." Think about that. Our daughters, sisters, nieces, and granddaughters are protecting themselves from the predatory actions of other teens and even predatory adults. And it's not because they are trying to avoid this type of aggressive and one-sided sexual experience. They already "know" and accept that it will happen to them. They're just trying to prepare themselves for it. Trying to protect their brains from the lifelong trauma of those experiences by watching videos showcasing what they may be hours away from experiencing. What event would have to be happening to you, four to six hours from now, that you would have to watch videos to prepare yourself for just to try to minimize the trauma you'll be burdened with after the fact? Would you be fighting Mike Tyson? Wrestling a grizzly bear? Fighting off a starving mako shark? This is what our kids think sex is supposed to be, and porn has taught them that.

In the interviews that I have done with teenagers, all of whom had started watching porn at around age eleven, they said the same thing: they started compulsively watching porn because no one told them they shouldn't. None of them currently have millions of followers on social media like Eilish, but their sentiments and stories were exactly the same. Just like Eilish, after years of this taboo issue being swept under the rug, they felt the need to talk to and encourage parents to discuss pornography with their children.

Overstimulation and Desensitization

One easily identifiable physical challenge that pornography viewing has for young people is the dramatic increase in arousal problems. Pornography-induced erectile dysfunction (PIED) and arousal deficiency damage the sexual pleasure of men and women. Because porn can depict such overly stimulating and fantasy-like images, when it comes time to engage sexually with a live human, it's difficult to become aroused, let alone achieve orgasm. As with drugs like heroin or cocaine, when your body gets flooded with dopamine, it sets the bar too high for common pleasures (such as watching a sunrise, doing well on a test, or spending time with loved ones) to compete with. These non-drug experiences do provide some dopamine as well, but the amount is no longer enough to satisfy the body that has gotten used to extreme levels of this hormone.

If you watch online pornography for years on end before you engage with a real person, your expectations for that encounter could be so far removed from reality that your body wouldn't physically respond to the natural stimulation that engagement with another human being can provide (Park et al. 2016). This is one of the saddest elements of this challenge for young people. Imagine being young and apprehensive about your own sexuality and finally getting up the courage to ask someone out. Let's say the date goes well, the relationship is going well, and you decide to engage with this person in an intimate way. You agree to take the relationship to the next level. Imagine if your physical body let you down every time, and you did not know why. It's embarrassing and frustrating for you. It could be embarrassing for your partner, who may wonder if they did something wrong or if you don't find them attractive. It could also alter your experience of relationships or sexuality for years to come, maybe even the rest of your life. And imagine if you experienced all of that hurt simply because a parent did not talk to you about porn in advance.

When I was in high school, boys made sure they always had a notebook or a textbook with them to hide an erection that could be caused by simply seeing an older upper-class girl—or by the mere thought of a girl—in a close-fitting sweater or tight pants. Boys would fantasize about what a girl looked like without her clothes on, and this would provide more than enough stimulation for a potentially unexpected erection. Today, rates of erectile dysfunction are through the roof. Imagining someone naked, or even being right next to someone naked, is now no longer enough stimulation to elicit the natural reaction one would expect. High school-age boys are buying erectile dysfunction pills online and suffering through something during adolescence that historically boys in my day might have experienced maybe a handful of times in their whole lives.

Years ago, almost two years after doing an in-home coaching session with a family, the mom reached back out and said that her nineteen-year-old son who attended the session when he was seventeen wanted to speak with me alone. I usually don't do that, but with the proper papers signed, I agreed to have this young man come to my office without his parents present. There, he told me the saddest story I have ever heard. I wanted to share it with you here so that you can (if you choose to) share it with your children.

This young man, let's call him Aiden, told me that while he was home from college for the summer he ran into "Sarah," a friend from high school who he liked and who (unbeknownst to him) had also liked him. They had never connected in high school other than as friends, and they were both glad to run into each other out at a party. Both were home from their freshman year of college. While they were home, they dated for a while and liked each other, but both knew they were going to go back to separate colleges in the fall. While they were home, one thing led to another, and over the summer they agreed that they were going to have sex with each other. Everything I was hearing seemed natural and pleasant so far.

Sarah's parents were going to be out of town for a couple of days at one point, so Aiden told his parents he was going to go hang out with a friend and went to Sarah's house. This gave them a whole evening to actually take their time to "fool around." They were making out on the couch and started undressing one another. Aiden was having fun, and so was Sarah at this point. But when it came time to take off Aiden's pants, he realized he didn't have an erection, even with all the kissing and groping he'd been doing with a girl he liked personally and was physically attracted to.

"It sucked," Aiden told me, explaining how embarrassing it was and how it changed the entire interaction in a terrible way. He was putting on a brave face, but it had really freaked him out, and he remained scared about it even while we were talking.

"Okay," I said, "it happens sometimes. It's nothing to worry about."

Aiden told Sarah that his stomach hurt as a way to save face, and he left her house.

I thought the story was over, hoping this was just a one-off occurrence. But this painful moment with Sarah was only the beginning, a symptom of a larger issue.

"It was the weirdest thing," Aiden told me, "because when I went home I was able to masturbate when I watched porn." I could tell Aiden was really scared about not being able to have sex with Sarah. His confidence was shot, and he was really worried that this was a permanent problem. I knew he wanted me to tell him it would all be okay, and I did. I told him to stop watching porn and that problem should go away. But it can take many months for the brain and body to start to "reset" back to a mode that allows common arousal cues like kissing someone or touching their breasts or undressing them to have the same impact they would without the influence of regular porn viewing. Unfortunately, most kids wouldn't wait that long before they started watching porn again.

In many conversations I have had with young people in family coaching sessions, young teens said that they would rather send compromising pictures of themselves to each other than hold hands because holding hands is "weird." Physical touch with someone they like is weird. Sending a photo of their privates or of themself naked is easy. The process of meeting someone, impressing them with your wit, spending time with them, discovering their interests, and then exploring your sexuality gradually is awkward for today's youth, even nonexistent. These experiences have now mostly disappeared from our children's developmental landscape. Yet these are also the very experiences that they need to build the bonding mechanisms necessary for healthy, long-term romantic and social relationships.

Porn Addiction

Research from 2011 revealed that by the time boys were fourteen or fifteen they might have been viewing as many as six or seven videos a day and may have seen 15,000 explicit adult videos by the time they left high school. If your child saw 15,000 videos on how to build a deck or cook a turkey for Thanksgiving, they would be an expert. Hands down. There would be no reason for them to go to school to learn how to build a deck or cook a turkey. Fifteen thousand videos are enough for anyone to become an expert on anything.

But because the videos kids are watching rarely depict realistic, healthy sexual encounters, they aren't becoming experts on being a wonderful sexual partner (understanding consent, considering the sexual needs of their partners, etc.). They are just becoming experts on viewing various kinds of pornography. Because watching porn fires the same receptors in the brain as injecting heroin or snorting cocaine, it is all too easy for kids to develop an addiction. In its most basic form, an addiction is a compulsion to do something that hurts you. So even though they aren't getting enough sleep, are falling behind in school, and have stopped hanging out with their friends, a child may continue to obsessively watch porn because their brain is being rewarded with bursts of dopamine. Humans are wired to seek out and repeat behaviors that provide dopamine boosts. This includes activities like eating food, sleeping, and having sex. That's why these behaviors feel good to us. These actions have helped us survive as a species. But in today's world, we have easy access to many ways of quickly getting our bodies to release vast amounts of dopamine, including watching videos on social media, eating high-sugar foods, playing video games, and using recreational drugs. Watching porn belongs on this list as well.

When we can get high levels of pleasure from something with virtually no effort (i.e., tapping a screen a few times to get to a porn site), we're more likely to repeat that behavior so we can get those chemical rewards again. Many adults are not even self-aware enough to understand that they have fallen into an addiction. Even when people confront them about it, they struggle to see how the addiction (to drugs, a relationship, gambling, etc.) is problematic. This is partially because the promise of a big dopamine hit clouds their judgment and confuses their perspective on the situation. So if adults struggle, children stand essentially no chance of recognizing and getting help for a porn addiction without a parent or other caring adult stepping in.

With the phone they carry in their pocket or the tablet in their backpack, headphones firmly in place, they can watch porn in math class, on the school bus, at their friend's house, or on their own in their room. And they can do it without drawing any undue attention to themselves, because who doesn't see dozens of kids with earbuds in walking around looking at their phones all day?

Imagine if your child's phone came filled with a never-ending supply of heroin and a needle, like a stylus, that was embedded in the phone. Would you want your child to have access to the app that lets them shoot up while they're at school or at home? Would you allow your child to get free heroin whenever they want, in whatever quantities they want? What I want to be sure you understand is that, even though you and I know the difference between internet pornography and a drug like heroin, your child's brain has no clue. All it knows is that whatever the kid did to get that jolt of dopamine needs to happen again, and soon.

If, after a conversation with your young person, you discover this is a bigger problem than you may have imagined, get them help. If you have a hospital or other facility in your area that helps with addictive diseases, get your child the help they need as soon as possible. If you're uncertain about where to turn, you can contact the Substance Abuse and Mental Health Services Administration (SAMHSA) hotline at 1-800-662-4357 or Sex Addicts Anonymous at 1-800-477-8191. These numbers will link you to people in your area who can help you find the professional support you need to get your child healthy.

Just like being diagnosed with cancer or developing diabetes, becoming addicted to pornography is nothing to be ashamed of. Again, the confluence of availability, interest, and access, combined with a lack of any meaningful conversation from parents or other caring adults, is simply not a child's fault. The shame and guilt are part of the problem. Getting professional help may be the best route to take. It may take multiple months for you to start to see improvement in their condition and multiple years before it seems like they are back to their normal selves. Just like you were willing to be uncomfortable for them, be willing to be patient and see their recovery through. It'll be tough, but they can get better. People all over the world begin to recover from porn addiction every single day.

Sexual Assault

While I understand and celebrate that young people exploring their own sexuality is a healthy part of childhood, our kids are not playing "doctor" anymore. Our children, at very young ages, are copying what they see in porn movies because they are not being taught any other alternative. They are simply a product of their current environment.

Some of the saddest conversations I have had are with young girls. They will describe their initial sexual exposure and recount to me that, looking back to when they were age sixteen or seventeen, they now believe that their first (sometimes their first several) sexual interactions were instances of assault. When they look back on those memorable moments, it is not the innocent fumbling of learning how to kiss or the awkwardly wonderful first experience of holding hands with a sweaty palm. It is not the thrill or excitement of sharing something special with a person who they think is great and who thinks they are great. It is the realization that what that person did "to them" (not with them) was far beyond what they were expecting, what they were interested in, or what they would have agreed to if they had been asked. But they were afraid to speak up because that was how "all the boys" behaved in their school or their grade (and in schools and grades across the country). But with more experience and a healthier perspective, they look back and believe, if they are honest with themselves, that they were sexually assaulted.

Watching porn can mean viewing videos in which people are blackmailed, threatened, and verbally and physically abused until they do what the other character wants, regardless of how painful, humiliating, or dangerous it might be. As noted in the section on healthy sex, porn sites often show the exact opposite of healthy sex. There is often no attempt to get consent from the other partner, or the refusal is blatantly ignored. This is an example of unethical sex being depicted. There is often what's called "taboo" sex taking place, which can include someone playing the role of a child (stepdaughter, nephew, cousin, etc.) having sex with someone playing the role of an adult (father, aunt, coach, etc.). This would be a depiction of illegal sex.

If a child grows up watching this for years, it stands to reason that they would come to believe that this is how sex is done. So when they go to have their first sexual encounter with someone, they may think nothing of forcing themselves on their partner, dismissing their hesitant body language or even their verbal "No" as part of the experience of sex. Because the actors they see online do this while playing their roles, it could be seen as a playful way to be coy or that they don't really mean it and are just shy. Without anyone to explain that porn videos are actors playing roles, the perpetrator of sexual assault (not to excuse their actions, mind you) may honestly have no idea that what they've done counts as assault (the same way that some people don't realize in the moment that what was done to them constituted assault).

Our kids are growing up with hidden cameras secretly filming their first innocent interactions and then having them posted on social media for the world to see. They are growing up with sex bracelets. They are growing up with boyfriends who share pictures or videos taken secretly or intentionally as leverage or "revenge" against a potential breakup. They are growing up with AI placing their face on the body of a porn actor and that video being sent around their school, family, or workplace as a joke. They are growing up with a hundred million sexual images and videos available to them in their back pockets, three taps away on their phone. This all makes it easy for sexual assault to seem normal.

Societal Problems

While the internet's ability to give people exactly what they're looking for in a matter of seconds plays a pivotal role in the horrible mental and physical problems that kids can experience from viewing internet pornography, there is more to this issue. This section outlines the ways in which people contribute to these issues. This includes society-wide beliefs and behaviors that serve to keep child porn exposure and the social impacts that child porn exposure has on kids hidden.

Seeing Porn as Sexual Education

It's easy for parents to think that porn is "just part of growing up," as if it somehow is the same as formal sexual education. But just because it exists doesn't mean it's helpful or harmless. This is similar to thinking that drug use or sexual assault or cancer are just part of growing up. Most parents wouldn't sit idly by while their child took fentanyl or was raped by their date or developed malignant growths in their bodies. They would step in to either prevent these things from happening or at least get treatment for them as soon as possible after discovering the problem (start a drug rehab program, get trauma-informed therapy, or start cancer treatments). I'm encouraging parents to do the same with internet porn exposure. Before reading this book, you wouldn't have had the awareness or tools to engage in effective prevention. I get that. But after reading this book, you can intervene on behalf of your children because you know how to do so by having had The Third Talk with them.

Think about learning about sex in comparison to learning how to drive. We have driver's education set up all across the country, run by professionals who understand how to safely operate motor vehicles. We teach safe driving in schools. Most parents and guardians have a valid driver's license and can adequately train their own teens to drive or reinforce what they learn in driver's education classes. We do this because the vast majority of kids will eventually drive. It is imperative for their safety to be taught how to do it well and to practice safe driving multiple times over the course of months or years and under the supervision of licensed drivers. We do this for the safety of our kids, their passengers, and the pedestrians, drivers, and cyclists they share the road with.

When it comes to sexual education, this would be the equivalent of having the "birds and bees" talk with your children, having a trained pediatrician talk to your children about anatomy, and having an experienced and qualified counselor or health teacher talk to your children about healthy human sexuality. You know they would receive accurate information in a safe environment where they could ask questions and be appropriately guided on respecting their partner and themselves during their sexual encounters. Parents would also be there to answer questions and (like driving) have the final say on all the rules. We require our children to spend about a year slowly learning to drive. How much time do you spend with your kids, or do our teachers spend with our kids, teaching them about healthy sexuality? My experience has been that parents spend about three hours total across their child's entire lifetime discussing healthy sexuality with them.

Children getting their sex education from online pornography is like them learning how to drive by watching a Fast and Furious movie. This exaggerated, dangerous, and unrealistic depiction of driving would only serve to put your child (and their passengers, pedestrians, and fellow drivers) in harm's way. The same goes for porn. What children find on porn sites is often a massive collection of images and recordings created by professionals who are play-acting various scenarios and adult fantasies. These clips rarely, if ever, have anything to do with two people who love and respect one another having loving, safe, healthy sexual interactions.

Discovering sex through the lens of pornography can be extremely shocking and even permanently traumatizing for a young person. The material they see can feature sexual objectification that diminishes the humanity of the performers. This can lead children to view people they may find interesting or attractive solely as two-dimensional sexual objects instead of people with thoughts, feelings, interests, and experiences of their own. Building a nonsexual relationship with someone and getting to know them is not part of many of the sexual encounters represented in online pornography. Yet the platonic side of romantic relationships is the single most important element that makes relationships last years and decades instead of just minutes or days. Without exercising the mental muscles necessary for dating someone (showing interest in them, carrying on a conversation, exploring commonalities and discussing differences, etc.), our kids are robbed of an opportunity to build the skills necessary for successful, long-term, healthy relationships of all kinds.

I grew up and went through puberty in a world without online porn. What I learned by dating, falling in love, and gradually exploring my own sexuality when I was young paved the way for every relationship I have had. I've learned how to hold a conversation, listen to someone else's point of view, and care about what it's like to interact with me as a boyfriend, father, or friend. Had I grown up with 100 million porn videos available to me at the press of a few buttons, I have no idea where I would be right now. With my experience watching this content tear holes in the fabric of many families, I can say without reservation, if I had grown up with internet porn as my sexual education, I would not have been better, healthier, or happier than I am now.

Choosing Profits Over Protection

Porn is easily and effectively distributed via the internet. Sites like Patreon, DeviantArt, and Only Fans make the list of top ten most visited sites for adult content, but Pornhub, XVideos, and XNXX hold the top three spots for porn sites by most statistics. There is a web of industries that benefit from people searching for, viewing, and paying for pornography on these and other websites.

Internet service providers (ISPs) are the companies that you pay for access to the internet. As long as people want to pay their monthly fee for access, the ISP gets their money and they're satisfied, regardless of what customers are using that internet access to do. Cell carriers provide essentially the same thing, but with the ability to make phone calls and send text messages as well. But that mobile data can and is used to access pornographic material twenty-four hours a day, 365 days a year. And, again, as long as people are paying their phone bills, there isn't a lot of incentive to discourage customers from doing something like watching porn with however much data they have on their plan.

Search engines also get massive numbers of searches every second of every day for porn images and videos by people all over the world. They get paid when people use their service to search for information online because they show ads within and alongside the provided results. So, again, as long as people are using their search engine to find whatever they are looking for (including pornography), they don't have much reason to try to steer people away from pornographic material.

Pornographic content creators, of course, get paid to continue creating their content. There is a high demand for it. While some may offer subscription services, others may post their content for free and then make money from advertisements on their page, product placement, or even commercials within their video pointing viewers to more expensive content or a product they're an affiliate for. As long as people (they have no way of knowing the age of anyone viewing their content) continue to search for what they create, view it, and pay for it, they have no strong incentive to stop creating the content. Pornography is an industry that is globally worth nearly $100 billion annually. To put that into perspective for you, that's a little less than Bill Gates's 2024 estimated net worth of just over $131 billion, but it's not an amount that porn has accumulated over the course of a lifetime or even a few decades. The industry earns that much money every single year, again and again and again.

"Fixing" Children's Bodies

There are hundreds of studies that show that young girls with a poor body image will engage in riskier behavior and may use drastic methods of "correcting the problem" through cosmetic procedures (Kalampalikis & Michala 2023). These body images can be a result of seeing porn performers with bodies that cost tens of thousands of dollars to create. Watching these artificially crafted bodies can easily make people feel as if they don't "match up." Of course, this message is reinforced by the carefully curated videos that kids see daily from models on social media, on magazine covers, or in movies and on television shows. I'm horrified by the idea that thirteen-year-old girls are having procedures like breast augmentation to increase their bust size or labiaplasty to change the way their vagina looks. This is how watching porn can destroy their self-esteem. They are not broken and do not need "fixing." We all look different. We all matter. Our bodies are beautiful and should be respected and appreciated.

To refer back to the Fast and Furious example, we need to remind kids that it's okay (and normal, healthy, smart, and safe) to drive the speed limit in their own car (body) and obey the traffic laws (engage in healthy sexual behaviors). Actual driving on city streets may not be as fantastical as what happens in the movies, but it's the way the entire audience is going to drive home (and likely how the movie crew and actors all drove home after filming wrapped up!). In the same way, having loving sex with someone they care about may not be as exciting as the exaggerated acts that kids may see in a porn video, but it's the way that the vast majority of human beings have sex safely and enjoyably.

Focusing on Morality

Based on everything I've written about why and how children access pornography, it's clear that it has nothing to do with morality. Having gotten access to porn doesn't make them "bad" or "wrong" or "sinful." It just makes them flawed human beings like the rest of us. We need to shift away from a morality-based argument for preventing kids from watching pornography. When we make moral judgments, all we do is instill shame and guilt in our children and push them to not want to talk to us about the struggles that they are having with pornography. Making children feel that they are bad or unworthy because they have watched pornography is a very big part of the long-term problem. I believe that the potentially lifelong disgrace we create in our children when we judge them like this can be as harmful as the pornography itself. Using morality as a deterrent to watching this content can cause further pain for your child, but the one thing it doesn't do is solve any of the problems they are facing. It's one thing to make a mistake, but it's a whole other thing to be considered a terrible person because of your mistakes, especially at such a young age.

Instead, we need to work toward understanding and discussing our children's exposure to porn. And it helps to do that from the perspective that watching internet pornography is a brain-altering behavior that can have catastrophic health consequences for children and adolescents in every area of their lives. We need to talk about this as a national health challenge and not a moral failing on the part of our kids or their parents.

Shame can also keep parents from addressing porn in their own homes, churches, schools, and other community hubs. I think it has the opposite outcome from what the people labeling pornography as "immoral" may actually want to achieve. Most parents don't want to be seen as "bad," and they don't want their kids to be seen that way either. So in order to avoid that embarrassment, they just don't talk about it at all. I've already revealed to you how dangerous that is. Some people still believe that not addressing something means that it isn't there or that it will go away on its own. But that's not how this, or any other difficulty in life, works. Trying to ignore a problem just means that you don't get the help you need, not that it goes away. And your silence on the issue usually means that it just gets increasingly worse over time. Then, when it comes to a head in painful and public ways (for example, your kid being caught with a nude picture of a classmate at school and being charged with possession of child pornography, also known as child sexual abuse material, or CSAM), much more damage is done than if you had started a simple, initially awkward conversation with your children in the privacy of your own home.

While kids will encounter or engage with various people and organizations throughout their childhood, parents are usually the most consistent human beings in their lives. Parents will be around from preschool through college if health and finances work out. Since we know that the viewing of pornography often starts at age eleven or twelve, providing exposure prevention means talking to kids when they're about eight or nine years old, usually around third or fourth grade, well before middle school.

These early conversations can help them understand what to avoid and how. It will also signal to them that it's okay to talk to you about someone exposing them to pornography or any sex-related topic they can think of, including "the birds and the bees." It is ironic and sad that parents today need to have The Third Talk before they have historically had "the birds and the bees" talk. That change happened in the span of one generation, and we now need to adjust by talking honestly with our kids, not by shaming, blaming, or judging.

Punishing Instead of Guiding

As noted in previous chapters, a parent's knee-jerk reaction to believing or having it confirmed that their child is watching porn may be punishment. This can mean grounding, taking away a device like a phone or laptop, or abruptly canceling plans the child has their heart set on (prom, a party, a field trip, etc.). Sadly, this is many parents' response to almost any kind of unwanted behavior by their children. Yet, statistically, this is rarely beneficial to the child. In order to grow into someone who makes healthy decisions without someone supervising them, a person needs to understand what behavior is expected, why, and how to avoid failing to meet those expectations. I have never found that taking away a child's phone is a thoughtful deterrent. I have presided over conversations between parents and kids in which the child openly admits that they never brought up their daily obsessive porn watching for no other reason than because they knew the parent would take their phone away.

It is my belief that threatening to take away your child's phone or laptop can be so devastating to them that they will suffer through addiction, compulsion, social ostracization, mental health challenges, physical health challenges, assaults, and many other hurdles simply to be able to keep their phones. I think that threatening to take away your child's phone will backfire every time unless your goal is for your child to suffer in silence.

Instead, if you need a "deterrent," make it a requirement that you know every password and app on your child's phone, that you see their history every day, and that you know what they use their phone for. Having no history on their phone when they get home generally means that they wiped it clean and is solid confirmation that they've been watching porn. If your kids want to watch it, they will find a way.

I and my team at The Third Talk believe strongly that communication and conversation about your own family values is so important that we do not spend a lot of time discussing punishment in our lectures or school presentations. We do not suggest you utilize anyone's family values but your own. We do not suggest you use anyone's strategy for parenting but your own, and we do not make any claims about your family punishment approach either. What we offer here is that it has been our experience that punishment regarding internet pornography sets shame in motion and ends the opportunity for parents to be the trusted adult in whom a child can confide. If it's not safe to talk to you—the person who is supposed to love them most in the world—who can they talk to about this? That is scary for me as a parent to think about.

Grooming and Trafficking

One of the major problems with our children watching this content at such young ages is their belief that this content is an actual physical depiction of how adults behave sexually or how they should or will behave when they get older. There is a myriad of dangers that exist for our children because of this, but an important one for parents to understand is grooming. Grooming is how a predator convinces a young person that a physical interaction with them is acceptable. If a child has watched hundreds of videos showing a student having sex with a teacher, coach, priest, or other adult, it introduces that concept to them as being "okay." After all, everyone they see in the porn videos seems to be having fun, so it must not be that bad. This makes it so much easier for a predator to convince a child that it's okay to interact with them online (when they realize that the person they're chatting with in a forum is an adult, they don't break off communication), meet them in person without their parents knowing, and have sex with them and not tell anyone about it. Being able to so easily lead a child into this kind of thinking is just another negative result of children watching internet porn.

Social media and the desire for "likes" also plays a role here. Kids want to be seen as popular, and the desire to increase their circle of friends can lead to some scary interactions. And our children may not be mature enough to understand the real danger they are in. Loneliness plays a role. If your son or daughter is lonely (a common side effect of watching porn), it can make any attention, even inappropriate attention by adults they don't know, more appealing to them.

These predators aren't always only looking to victimize our children themselves. Sometimes they are setting up plans to meet in person in order to abduct the child and traffic them. During the pandemic, we saw a dramatic increase in sex trafficking across the country. Several law enforcement officials attribute this to our children being in front of their computers more often due to virtual learning. Being in front of their computers more often, and at such young ages, exposed children to pornography at a much higher rate during the pandemic. As we have just discussed, watching that much pornography makes children easier to groom by adults, and those adults are sometimes traffickers.

The grooming process can start eight months in advance of the actual trafficking or abduction of a child and begin as a simple request from an older person posing as a student in their school or a nearby school who then convinces your child that sending nude pictures or videos of themself is normal or "cool." Once the trafficker has that first image or video, there is a downward spiral where the trafficker requires their target to send them more (and ever increasingly graphic) images or videos. They do this to blackmail the victim by threatening to expose those images or videos to their family, classmates, or friends.

Imagine your child walking out the door one day and letting you know they're going to the mall with their friends to meet "Andrew" in person. You know they've been talking for months about this new friend they met online who is in the same grade as them and plays volleyball just like they do. Like you would on any other day, you remind them of their curfew, make sure they have their phone in case there's an emergency, and send them on their way without a second thought.

You've pressed about Andrew before. Your child readily showed you almost a year's worth of texts and DMs that follow the storyline that this is a friend who has a lot in common with your kid. But that's all part of the ruse. And your child may not be lying to you. They could genuinely believe that they have made a new connection within the world. This is how sophisticated these predators are. These are professional criminals, and your child could be worth hundreds of thousands of dollars to them, if they can get a hold of them.

When they do eventually meet with a child, traffickers often use drugs to secure your child's participation in human sex trafficking. It doesn't have to start out with drugs. It can also be money, clothing, rent, or any tangible commodity that can start a child down this path. Drugs can be used to incapacitate a victim and can keep children going back to "the life" even if they don't want to, or even after they are "out" or "saved" by law enforcement or their family. It's insidious.

A second way that trafficking is increased by your child's exposure to internet porn is by fueling demand. While any child can be trafficked, the vast majority of victims are female, and the vast majority of "clients" are male. What often happens is that watching porn gives the viewer a false idea of what sex is supposed to be like. They struggle in high school to find a girl who is willing to do what they see online. They may think that college girls or adult women will do those things. Then they find out that they don't either. Their next option may be to pay for someone to do the things they see on porn sites. This leads to them becoming the people who pay traffickers to use abducted victims however they want. And, of course, getting to do the things they've been fantasizing about since high school encourages these guys to come back again and again. Demand goes up, so the traffickers meet that demand by grooming and abducting more kids, and the cycle continues.

Using and Funding Failed Movements

I've had a front-row seat since 2002 to the failure of initiative after initiative to curb porn's influence on young people. What I've learned from this experience (watching everything else fail) may be the most valuable information I offer to parents to help them make the change that we as American parents all need to make. I can tell you what hasn't worked and save you time, money, and heartache.

I founded The Third Talk as a stand-alone entity in 2013. A summit was organized by the British government in an attempt to keep young British children from viewing online porn. The search engines, the porn industry, and the largest internet service providers (ISPs) in England were invited. I became aware of that meeting and wrote a letter to the British Department of Culture, Media, & Sport (DCMS). I offered that they had the wrong players in the room to solve this problem. My view was based on the hard and fast numbers that pointed to who had the most power to make real changes when it came to kids viewing porn, and it wasn't the groups they invited, the representatives from ISPs, search engines, and the porn industry. From a financial standpoint, as noted in the previous section, none of these entities have an effective method for making sure kids don't see pornography content, even if they were really focused on that. But, again, there's really no business incentive for them to care. As long as people keep using the internet service they pay for, using their search engine, and using their porn sites for their adult content, those companies are satisfied.

With none of these companies having any idea how to keep children away from this content, two days passed, a lot of hand wringing and shoulder shrugging happened, and the decision was made to send any inquiries for images of underage nude pictures to the FBI. This practice, however, was already in place. The agreement was also made to send queries for inappropriate images or videos (child sexual abuse material, or CSAM) to the National Center for Missing & Exploited Children (NCMEC). Again, this was in place before the meeting. Yet money was gifted, the promise of algorithm reconfigurations made, and hands shaken. I imagine all the adults in that meeting purported to have made great progress, or at least put a check mark in a box. However, the teens and preteens in Britain were still left on their own to manage their exposure to internet porn. Yet these kinds of meetings and inept strategies get used and funded again and again.

This made me realize that no one was actually addressing the real elephant in the room: that underage children are the largest viewing demographic of internet porn in the world. It made me understand that I had to address a global issue that, if not solved now, will still be causing problems twenty years down the road. I wanted then, and now, to help as many parents and children as I could.

I did not attend that meeting hosted by the DCMS. I in no way mean to demean them or throw shade at them, or at anyone who works to protect kids from this content. What I am saying is that it didn't work. It didn't work there; it didn't work here. It didn't work then. It's not working now. It is time to change our tactics from hoping or expecting someone else to do this for us or for a "technical" solution to appear. It's been twenty-five years.

Porn just simply "is" for our children, and sadly, we have to accept that, just like we accept that thunderstorms are part of the weather on Earth. We would waste a lot of time and resources trying to eliminate this part of our world. Instead, we seek shelter during thunderstorms to keep ourselves and our families safe. We accept the reality and deal with it accordingly. With a clear and easy solution like The Third Talk, we have a way to "shelter in place" in the midst of this storm of internet pornography exposure. But we need stop leaning on failed movements and actually use this tool of compassionate conversation on a global scale.

FAILING WITH LEGAL ARGUMENTS

Historically, all media produced under the general umbrella of pornography is protected by the First Amendment, the freedom of speech. Yet many people try to attack the producers, actors, and distributors who create and publish pornographic content. But just as this issue is not a moral one, it's also not a legal one. The production of pornography is not in itself a crime. Therefore, this approach has failed for years.

FAILING WITH FILTERS

Many modern devices come with the ability to block certain websites. Apps and content blockers exist online and have been created to "protect" kids. In my opinion, and after having spoken with hundreds of young children on this topic, filters and blockers simply do not work. If they did, we wouldn't see the explosion of this content exposure to our kids. While these tools may help parents feel better, it is only an illusion of safety. Filters are easily breached by our tech-savvy kids, meaning that exposure can happen even when the blockers are in place. And of course our kids just turn them back on when they're done in case their parents decide to check them. This goes for every electronic device that can have blockers installed. You would have to be watching those filters the entire time your children were home to catch them in the act. Who is really going to do that? And it's important to remember that there is no filter for a young child at a sleepover or on a school bus with a classmate who shows them porn.

Additionally, the overall message you send when trying to control your child's device can be problematic. Namely, the breach of privacy and trust. If we're trying to teach our children how to make healthy decisions for themselves (without anyone physically or digitally looking over their shoulders), filters and blockers do the opposite. They teach the child that it's someone else's responsibility to keep them safe. But not everyone they meet (friends, lovers, employers, etc.) is going to take on that responsibility. It makes more sense to help kids understand what's unhealthy and support them in making mature decisions early, to avoid those things even when we aren't with them or there is no filter on a particular device they're using. To protect the child, we need to make them aware of the danger and how and why they should avoid this content.

CHAPTER SUMMARY

● Teaching our kids to make healthy decisions means they'll be protected even when we're not around.

● Internet porn can and will change the way kids view each other, sex, and their own sexuality.

● Viewing online pornography is an issue of health and safety, not morality.

● Internet porn causes horrible mental and physical health problems.

● Putting all the money and effort we have into failed movements is a waste.

CHAPTER 5
Staying The Course

"I was uneducated, and I thought that through pornography I could learn how to satisfy my partners and how to make them want to be with me. And, unfortunately, that put me in some very dangerous situations. Every relationship that I had ended up becoming abusive sexually. And I fully believe that is because of porn."

"Sarah"
An underaged teen interviewed by The Third Talk.
Full interview available at TheThirdTalk.org.

CHAPTER OVERVIEW

• The Third Talk is a conversation, not a lecture.

• There are many benefits to having and continuing The Third Talk for both you and your child.

• Porn exposure can happen to all children, no matter their background or lifestyle.

• The Third Talk can help give kids the great life they deserve.

In this final chapter, I want to leave you with some notes on having The Third Talk that parents have found helpful to hear during coaching sessions. These tidbits are meant to encourage and inspire you as you continue having The Third Talk with your children throughout their lives.

The "S" Word

While facilitating a The Third Talk workshop in a middle school auditorium, one of the students in attendance with his parents asked a great question.

"What do you say or do when somebody just shows you porn?"

I knew what he was asking and was able to read into his question. What do you do if someone shows you porn and you don't want to see it, but you want to avoid it without seeming like a snitch or a wimp (every middle-schooler's nightmare)?

"Well, that depends," I said. "Are you cool with the 'S' word?"

Really, I was asking his parents, the teachers, and the administrators in the room. But by asking him, I was securing the audience of all the eleven- and twelve-year-old boys in this class.

"Do you mean 'stupid'?" he asked. Everyone, including myself, erupted into laughter. I by no means meant the "S" word was "stupid." I carefully looked around the room, everyone much more relaxed by the laughter. I looked at the students, the teachers, the administrators, and the parents and made a calculated decision. I calmly, casually, and matter-of-factly said back to this young man: "No. I mean the word 'shit.'"

He loved it. His eyes widened, everyone looked around, and we all laughed again. He could not believe that a grown man in a suit, in his school, would offer a legitimate swear word out loud at this school function. The parents looked at the teachers, the teachers looked at the administrators, and the administrators looked back at the parents. The parents and kids were now either amused or surprised in a good-natured way. The teachers and the administrators were pleasantly and gratefully surprised that the parents took it so well, and the kids perked up and listened intently.

"Uh . . .," the boy said, "Yeah, I guess."

"Okay, then. If someone tries to show you porn on their phone, just say, 'Get that shit outta here,'" and I motioned with my hand as if I were pushing something away from my face. There was renewed laughter, and the administrators' heart rates returned to normal. I continued on with the session, which went very well. I now use that story in every middle school presentation that I do. "Get that shit outta here!" is a phrase that a child can use in real life. If you don't like the word "shit," find something else that will work for you (i.e., "garbage," "nonsense," "crap," "junk," etc.). Personally, I'd rather have a child swear up a blue moon than ever be exposed to internet porn.

I think sometimes people are surprised that we can make these presentations funny. But it's okay to do what you can to make the conversation as fun and comfortable as possible. It's hard to listen to someone and process what they're saying to you when you're stressed out, scared, or anxious. Having this conversation in an environment that feels safe and friendly only serves to help your children openly engage with you so that you can make sure they are hearing you and absorbing what you have to say. The goal is for them to believe in the idea that porn is not something they should be watching. For them to carry that idea with them wherever they go throughout their lives. You can't be with your child every minute of every day. At some point or another, they are going to interact with other children and adults when you're not around. This will be at school, a playground, a volunteering opportunity, a relative's house, or on a website playing video games. These are the times it's most critical to make sure your child understands that you don't want them exposed to porn and why. Especially if someone tries to show it to them or they stumble across it accidentally. Our children must be given real-world tools that will work to help them avoid, or deal with, exposure when we are not around.

Yes, Your Kid Too

Some parents reading this book might be shaking their heads, thinking, "That could never happen to my Olivia." This mindset only leaves your child unprotected. People have the same thought when it comes to bullying ("Ava would never!"), drug use ("Ethan knows better than that."), and other issues that are common struggles for children and teens. Accepting that our child may make mistakes like getting drunk or being unkind to someone is not some kind of moral failing on our part or theirs. It's just part of growing up and learning to be a member of society. Kids won't always make the best decisions, or say the nicest things, or handle strong emotions in a mature way. But that doesn't mean they are incapable of learning. And if parents embrace the idea that their child is human and makes mistakes, then parents can begin addressing those issues and guiding their children to become better people.

The same goes for the conversation about pornography. You have to monitor and attend to every aspect of your children's well-being. You have to make sure they have food to eat and water to drink, get clothes to wear, have supplies for school, get the transportation they need, and have adequate medical care (and much, much more!). On top of all that, we are also supposed to be helping them grow into healthy adults who are productive members of society, are fun to be around, and treat other people with respect. It's a lot! And it can seem like keeping them safe from the dangers of online pornography exposure is just one more thing on a never-ending parental to-do list. But based on the amazement, gratitude, and relief that the parents I've worked with have experienced after first starting this conversation with their children, I can tell you it's worth it. Is it a little uncomfortable at first? Sure. Will some of the answers to the questions you'll ask surprise you? Probably. But will your child be healthier and happier because you believed that a little awkwardness was worth making sure they avoid the negatives that come with watching online porn? Absolutely.

Helping Yourself

I've spent the entire book talking about how we can help children live happier, healthier lives. And I know that their happiness is directly related to your own. There are other ways that having this talk benefits you as a parent even as it is helping your children.

Relief

In the moments after you finish your first discussion with your children about porn, the next thing that usually happens is that you feel a great weight lifted from your heart. I have had many parents reach out to me and say that they have been waiting to have this conversation for years within their family, even if they didn't realize it until I taught them about The Third Talk. They feel a profound sense of accomplishment, relief, and even joy. It's empowering to realize that you are providing your children with the tools to help manage themselves within their reality. Helping your child navigate the world they live in feels good.

New Skills

Having tough conversations may be second nature to some people. But for others, it's new territory. You may not have had such awkward exchanges with other adults, let alone your own children. But once you have The Third Talk with your child, you will have acquired a new skill that you can use in the rest of your parenting. You know how to be uncomfortable and do something in spite of that discomfort because you know it's worth it. That means you have discipline, resolve, and bravery. It also means you're a better listener for your child and a person who has compassion and respect for them when they are going through a tough time. We have heard from parents that having this talk opened up the ability to have all kinds of new conversations with their children. This includes talking about topics like alcohol use, dating, or curfew. Parents can also be stronger listeners and offer patient, compassionate guidance when mistakes are made or problems arise, such as a messy breakup or getting drunk.

New Knowledge

Because there is no way for you to directly experience what being a teenager is like these days, you're going to learn a tremendous amount about that experience from your child. The more you listen, the more your child will speak, and the more they will teach you about the differences between how you grew up and how they are growing up. This understanding of a different perspective will help you become a better parent. It will help you become a more caring adult for the young people you come across in your life. This includes other kids you care for, such as your neighbor's children, church members, students, or coworkers.

Kids Deserve This

Think of The Third Talk as a capstone to the first sex talk. After a few hours of sex ed at school, our young people are then left on their own to explore their own sexuality, which they almost universally do online. With no one consistently telling them "This isn't good for you," curiosity gets the best of them and leads them further down this dangerous rabbit hole.

The Third Talk works so well simply because it is focused on health and safety, not blame and judgment. It's about having an ongoing, open dialogue about what kids are being exposed to. After all, you can't fix a problem you don't know is there. And even once you know it's an issue, you can't address it if you decide not to talk about it. After reading this book, if you have not spoken about it, or decide not to, that is a choice you are making. If I'm the first person to let you know online porn is a major issue for most teens and tweens, your child will be the second person to tell you that, no matter how indirectly. I don't think I could name a Billie Eilish song. That does not keep me from being profoundly grateful for and proud of her bravery. She is strong and smart and kind enough to tell us her story. Now we need to use her example and go speak with our own children.

All Hands on Deck

The Third Talk isn't just meant for the same-sex adults in a child's life, the parent who has the closer relationship with a child, or the parent who sees the child more often. Where there are two or more adults in the home (mom, dad, granny, uncle, older sibling, etc.), all the adults should be on the same page about the importance of addressing this issue with the younger people in the house. Be open to sharing this book or even reading it aloud to the other adults in your book group or community or in the home. Even summarizing what you've read is better than never discussing this topic with the people who are helping you raise your children on a day-to-day basis. Making sure the adults in a child's life are all on the same page about this issue only increases the protection for that child.

It's Up to Parents

It would be so much easier to pawn this problem, and the work that needs to be done to fix it, off on someone else. If we could pick a company, Google as an example, and make them the responsible party for eliminating childhood porn exposure. With the company fielding 95 percent of all search engine queries worldwide, we could say that Google allows our children to search for porn and then receive a result quickly and easily. Surely Google is aware that searches for porn increase 4,700 percent in the hours after school lets out (Net Nanny, 2017). Google is to blame for our children watching porn. Right?

Well, the answer is "sort of." Yes, Google gives people a way to find what they're looking for on the internet. But if someone never looks for porn in the first place, they aren't likely to find it. So the crux of the issue is helping kids understand that porn isn't healthy for them. But Google doesn't care about childhood porn exposure enough to fund getting The Third Talk facilitated multiple times per year in your community. Google gets data to sell and advertising revenue regardless of who makes a search query. It doesn't benefit Google to put time and energy into keeping children safe from internet porn.

Adults outside the home often have trouble getting permission from parents for basic sex education. It can be a struggle just to cover what kids need to know about pregnancy prevention, menstruation, and sexually transmitted infections. So getting clearance from parents to talk about porn in schools, at churches, or during scout troop or sports team meetings is likely a bit too far. So who's left?

Parents.

The caring adults who raise and guide kids throughout their lives. These are the people who are in the best position to help kids learn to prevent or manage their exposure to pornography. Since The Third Talk is a continuous process of small conversations about internet porn exposure, who better to facilitate that discussion than someone who interacts with the child on a consistent basis in their own home?

While it would be more comfortable and easier on us as parents to be able to lay this burden on someone else's shoulders, there's no one else who has the influence in a child's life that we do. It's up to us to take advantage of that fact and use it to protect our kids from harm.

CHAPTER SUMMARY

• Talking with your children about porn doesn't have to be a stuffy, boring, or overly serious experience.

• It's okay to find moments of levity during The Third Talk.

• Any child, no matter who they are or where they live, can be exposed to pornography.

• Having this conversation has benefits for you as a parent.

• We owe our kids The Third Talk because they deserve to be happy and live healthy lives.

• The Third Talk works even better as a family-wide (or community-wide) movement with all caring adults on board.

• It's up to parents to use The Third Talk to keep kids safe from exposure to internet pornography.

CONCLUSION

If every parent or caregiver across the country decided that it is now socially acceptable to talk to our children about prevention of online pornography exposure, and they also spoke to each other as parents about it, we could solve the problem of childhood exposure to internet pornography in a year or two. We as parents could feel good about something we all accomplished together, and an entire generation of children would be spared the psychological, social, and physical harm that exposure to pornography can cause.

American adults seem to generally be on the same page about the issue of childhood exposure to porn. In more than two decades of doing this work, I have never come across anyone who has argued on the opposite side of what I've said in this book. That would mean supporting the idea that children should be exposed to porn as early as possible. No one is promoting this perspective because people generally know that it's harmful and that they would never want their own, or other people's, children to be hurt by exposure to porn.

Parents and caregivers can often disagree on how to educate kids about sex, how to handle bullying online, or when a child should be allowed to date or even have a social media account. But this is one topic that every adult who cares about kids can agree on. Kids should not watch porn! We need to keep kids safe from exposure to online pornography. We need to teach them how to protect themselves in the moments we're not around. We need to agree and understand that this is a battle worth fighting for the kids we love.

And when we get to a point where we all openly and actively

teach our children that watching pornography online is not okay, the same way we have taught them that topics like drinking and dating are important to discuss, our entire world will become a better, safer place for our kids. We won't have to worry or wonder about how Caden's mom feels about her child watching porn. We won't have to be concerned with whether or not our kid knows how to say "Get that shit outta here!" when they need to. We can rest easy in the knowledge that our entire community is one that supports kids avoiding online pornography and that our world is full of parents who will alert us when there's been exposure of some kind. And they'll do that without shame, blame, or accusation.

Building a community like that within our familes, neighborhoods, and cities is worth two minutes of an awkward silence between you and your child. This is a movement! We need all parents in this fight, and we're not going to recruit them by trying to sweep the problem under the rug. Talk to your kids for a few minutes now instead of having them spend hours in therapy each month because they've developed a compulsive pornography habit they cannot break.

Talk to your kids for free now instead of paying court fees and missing work because you have to attend a hearing where your child, through sharing pictures, is being charged with possessing CSAM or distributing pornography to minors. Or they are charged with committing sexual assault. Or they are groomed, abducted, and trafficked by someone they met online. I know that may sound ridiculous to some, but trust me, it happens every single day. It happens to kids who have internet access. Period. Doesn't matter if they are getting online on their smartphone in their Beverly Hills mansion bedroom or if they are using the free Wi-Fi at their local library in their poverty-stricken neighborhood. It doesn't matter if they are obedient and get fantastic grades or if they're rebellious and a missed class away from flunking out of school. If your child has access to the internet anywhere, they are at risk.

We've all got to do something about this problem that's affecting our children as a generation. Having The Third Talk is a free, fast, simple way to solve this issue within your own home. Do it because it's the right thing to do. Do it because the future health and happiness of your children depend on it. Do it because it's what your kids deserve.

APPENDIX
Learning Beyond The Third Talk

Many people and organizations have addressed how hurtful and damaging internet pornography can be. What is new here at The Third Talk is that we are offering a real solution that has worked for many years. Not simply shaking our fist and saying how bad the problem is, but actually setting out to solve it with communication. This appendix is a collection of support resources, quotes, articles, and studies to help you begin your path to learning more about the qualitative and quantitative evidence surrounding this topic.

Information Hubs

American Association of Sexuality Educators, Counselors & Therapists (ASSECT): Early notions for many of our young kids today come through exposure to pornography, which includes dangerous ideas about using women for sexual satisfaction without regard for the needs of the woman. "If the kids are to have a knowledge of healthy sexuality, these early notions must be eliminated and replaced by ideas of appropriate touch and the joys of such touch, which is healthy sexuality." https://www.aasect.org/vision-sexual-health

Centers for Disease Control and Prevention (CDC): The evidence for SV [sexual violence] is still developing, and more research is needed. The problem of SV is too large and costly and has too many urgent consequences to wait for perfect answers. There is a compelling need for prevention now and to learn from the efforts that are undertaken. Commitment, cooperation, and leadership from numerous sectors, including public health, education, justice, health care, social services, business/labor, and government, can bring about the successful implementation of this package. https://www.cdc.gov/violenceprevention/pdf/SV-Prevention-Technical-Package.pdf

Department of Health and Human Services (DHHS): Sexual health is an intrinsic element of human health and is based on a positive, equitable, and respectful approach to sexuality, relationships, and reproduction that is free of coercion, fear, discrimination, stigma, shame, and violence. It includes the ability to understand the benefits, risks, and responsibilities of sexual behavior; the prevention and care of disease and other adverse outcomes; and the possibility of fulfilling sexual relationships. https://www.ncbi.nlm.nih.gov/pmc/articles/PMC3562741

The Third Talk: The Third Talk website is filled with articles, videos, links, and other resources to help you better understand pornography and its effect on kids as well as how to better support them in not consuming it. I've been working for decades to help schools, churches, recreation centers, scout troops, and other places where children gather become safe spaces for accurate information about pornography and its dangers. I encourage parents to visit the website to help them start their own conversations with their children about avoiding pornography. School administrators can work with The Third Talk to develop regular programming related to keeping kids away from this damaging content. Youth-group leaders can also work with our team to set up programming that will allow the young people they work with to get the education they need about staying away from pornography. Reach out to us on www.thethirdtalk.org or email us at info@thethirdtalk.org. We'd love to help and look forward to hearing from you.

World Health Organization (WHO): One of the most effective ways to improve sexual health in the long term is a commitment to ensuring that adolescents and young people are sufficiently educated to make healthy decisions about their sexual lives. Accurate, evidence-based, appropriate sexual health information and counseling should be available to all young people and should be free of discrimination, gender bias, and stigma. Such education can be provided via schools, workplaces, health providers, and community leaders.

https://apps.who.int/iris/bitstream/handle/10665/70501/WHO_RHR_HRP_10.22_eng.pdf?sequence=1

From Our Participants and Partners

We invite anyone who has attended or been influenced by any of The Third Talk sessions to let us know how it worked for them. We've posted some of these videos and statements on our website. Some are from children and teens who are sharing their experiences with pornography, sexual assault, porn addiction, and other issues. Others are from parents who want to share what it was like to have The Third Talk with their children, including the relief and hope that comes with getting the subject out in the open. Another set of testimonials are from professionals (teachers, police officers, government officials, etc.) regarding the impact that The Third Talk has had on the problem of children being exposed to pornography.

"I have worked in law enforcement for over twenty-four years and have seen all kinds of bravery. Standing up in a room full of people to address a topic that has been mostly ignored is brave, especially a topic as provocative as online viewing of explicit adult material by young people. John is brave. John has put his name and reputation on the line publicly to assist our parents and their children to defend against a huge and mostly silent challenge for our children; namely, the volume of pornography kids view at very early ages. When I first went to see John's presentation, I did not know what to expect. However, his delivery and command of the facts and statistics surrounding

this challenge were well presented and easy to hear. He immediately took all the fear and trepidation out of the room and was very easy to listen to. I would encourage teachers, and especially parents, to reach out to John and have him speak to their young people. His talk is not accusatory or scary; on the contrary, it is insightful and thought-provoking. I believe in John and his bravery, and that is exactly what we need to address this topic. On a personal note, I have found John to be personable, warm, and funny and genuinely interested in others. I would recommend him and his talk to everyone interested in protecting children and preventing harm. I highly endorse him, and I am constantly recommending anyone who is interested, or even those who are apprehensive about this topic, to come and listen to John's presentation."

Major Robert Ramirez – Investigations Commander,
Fayetteville Police Department

"John did a presentation at (school) last year that was such a big hit, parents personally funded him repeating it a couple of months later so even more could hear his crucial message. He has a way of handling a tough and anxiety-producing topic with grace, authenticity, and even humor, making us appropriately concerned for how important this issue is, while also empowering us with tools and confidence to address it with our kids. The real talent is engaging the teens themselves that are also invited to attend. As one said afterward, 'Honestly, it was the last thing in the universe I wanted to go to with my parents, and I'm actually really glad I did. We would've never talked about it otherwise… and we really need to.' I highly recommend him!"

Kriya Lendzion, MA, NCC, LPC, LCAS

"I have had the pleasure of working with John Van Arnam on the Male Engagement Committee of the North Carolina State PTA. When I first learned about John's topic, prevention of exposure to this material for young people, I was hesitant to commit to offering my assistance. I believe that I, like most parents, was apprehensive about how this topic could be delivered to parents and young people at the same time and how anyone could offer this discussion in a way that would not be offensive. That is, until I met and worked with John. John's delivery is so straightforward and easy to hear that you quickly move past any "awkward" nature of the topic itself and move quickly and effortlessly to his solution, which is also very

straightforward and easily understood. John does not point fingers or place blame, nor does he discuss body parts, website names, or any of the other perceived wording one might expect or fear from having this conversation. I am not 100 percent sure how he does it, but I am very glad he does. I give John my highest recommendation as a speaker and as a prevention professional. As I have gotten to know John, I also find him to be a good person with a good heart. Our state needs more people like John to simply roll up their sleeves and tackle a difficult discussion with grace, care, and humor."

Dr. Leroy Wray, Director of Teacher Recruitment and Retention UNCA/Lecture Professor at several UNC universities

"The research-based talk that John presented shed unexpected light on the pervasiveness, developmental implications, and critical need to talk directly about the subject in a way that was accessible and enjoyable to youth, parents, and professionals. John revealed the likely inevitable experiences that youth may encounter through peer or other social interactions, and he gave tangible tools for parents to develop confidence in communicating with their students about strategies to stay safe. Parents and youth were particularly moved to conversation and action following John's follow-up workshop where a young woman shared her firsthand account of her exposure to unsafe content and long-term impacts. By hosting the events, students reported a benefit of being able to talk more openly about their personal experiences with their parents and their increased confidence in setting boundaries with peers engaged in viewing harmful content. As a school counselor and mental health professional, I look forward to inviting John to ongoing events to guide our community."

Tiffany Mead - LCSW, LCAS School Counselor

"The Third Talk is important because it is hard to find an individual this program will not impact. Peer pressure is real. Friends see things; they share it with their friends. I think it's so important to utilize this tool to help and really try to get in front of this problem and be a part of the solution. I would 100 percent recommend giving The Third Talk an opportunity to come to your school and really let the program do what it does best and impact the lives of not only parents but children for the good."

Austin Bailey, Public Relations Coordinator

Thomas Jefferson Classical Academy

"We appreciate you coming and sharing your expertise with us. Your presentation was well received by parents and students. It was shared in a nonjudgmental way and provided parents with tools needed to help support their children. Parents appeared to be appreciative of learning more about a topic that is often taboo. I left the presentation feeling hopeful that parents would start having conversations with their children at home about pornography, around the dangers and risks of watching online pornography. I am thankful for you and the work you are doing. I hope that your message continues to be heard by parents in our local community and across the country."

Lindsey Foster, LCSW - Middle School Counselor

"I think The Third Talk lends itself perfectly to [arming parents with the tools they need to address this challenge]. [John gives] everyone in attendance an easy road map . . . I think it's important for us to face our fears as a society. We have to hit this epidemic head on. As administrators, it's time that we face the reality and face the truth that we need help. We need help with this topic, and we need to do a much better job for our young people to help save them and put them in a better place. They are learning [sexuality] from all the places we don't want them to learn it from."

Dr. Devon Carson, Principal, Guilford Preparatory Academy

"As a 25-year K–12 educator, I fully endorse The Third Talk and John Van Arnam's work on unfettered access to pornography and inappropriate internet content. John's dogged focus on pornography/ inappropriate internet content as the "root cause" of most of the social challenges of our middle and high school students is so very important to everyone who works on raising our youth: parents, educators, and clergy alike. Bullying, aggression (physical and psychological), shaming, fear, and personal and sexual devaluation are the outward symptoms we see that can be directly connected to pornography and inappropriate internet content. The term "root cause" denotes the deepest, lowest, earliest, most basic cause for a given behavior, most often a problematic behavior. The issue at hand is that most of our current educational programs focus on the symptoms because the root cause, pornography, requires a terribly uncomfortable conversation

most of us can't bring ourselves to have and a level of self-reflection that can bring into question our morals and values. To connect the root cause analogy, it is like using a weed-eater to make the yard look good and then wondering why the weeds grow back within a few days. We all know that, until we dig up the roots, the yard will remain full of weeds. Getting the hand implements, or sometimes just using our hands, to dig the weeds out by the roots and eradicate them is much harder work, but if we want the yard to look permanently good, we have to do that work. John is doing that work. If we want our kids to be healthy, we have to be willing to take on the root cause of the problem directly, and that is why I fully endorse John's program. The GREAT news is that John and the Third Talk Team are here to make it as easy as possible. I am very excited about doing everything I can to make sure that as many schools, students, parents, and educators as possible across the country have the tools, training, and assistance they need to do this work, and offering them The Third Talk is the way to do that!"

Jeff Litel – Director of Special Projects, State and Federal Programs

"I had the pleasure of working with John to develop a comprehensive school safety resource guide for the North Carolina Department of Public Instruction. His knowledge on child safety issues was invaluable to the project's success and to the parents and educators who received that information. His message about the dangers of online pornography is powerful and impactful, not only for the vast expertise he brings to the issue, but for his fun, genuine, and candid approach, which undoubtedly sparks much-needed, healthy conversations between parents and their children."

Dr. Jennifer Watson, Educator

You can find more testimonials at www.thethirdtalk.org/testimonials.

Articles

Modern Pornography

- https://community-matters.org/2020/01/22/sexual-misconduct-in-our-schools-students-hold-key/

- http://www.nbcnews.com/id/39650828/ns/technology_and_science-science/t/history-pornography-no-more-prudish-present/#.XQZxrf5MGCh

- https://stream.org/sexual-revolution-50-aged-like-harvey-weinstein/

- https://www.huffpost.com/entry/parenting-in-the-digital-age-of-pornography_b_9301802

- https://inspiyr.com/pornography-addiction-increases-with-tech-reliance/

- https://www.cnbc.com/2017/08/29/us-addresses-internet-addiction-with-funded-research.html

- https://www.businessinsider.com/how-porn-drives-innovation-in-tech-2013-7

- https://www.digitaltrends.com/computing/what-is-the-dark-web/

- https://nypost.com/2017/09/07/your-cell-phone-porn-habit-isnt-as-secret-as-you-think/

- http://theconversation.com/virtual-reality-could-transform-pornography-but-there-are-dangers-78061

- https://www.sciencedirect.com/science/article/pii/S0925231217312493

- https://www.yourbrainonporn.com/philip-zimbardo-the-demise-of-guys-2011

- https://www.semrush.com/trending-websites/global/adult

Societal Impact

- https://bigthink.com/videos/alva-noe-on-why-pornography-is-not-art

- https://www.newstatesman.com/culture/2013/06/can-pornography-be-art

- https://www.theatlantic.com/national/archive/20ten/03/pros-and-cons-of-porn/346134/

- https://en.wikipedia.org/wiki/Legal_status_of_internet_pornography

- http://marripedia.org/effects_of_pornography

- https://www.webroot.com/us/en/resources/tips-articles/internet-pornography-by-the-numbers

- http://www.techaddiction.ca/files/porn-addiction-statistics.jpg

- https://www.yourbrainonporn.com/ybop-articles-on-porn-addiction-porn-induced-problems/effects-of-porn-on-the-user/young-porn-users-need-longer-to-recover-their-mojo/

Pornography & Underage Consumption

- https://www.sciencedirect.com/science/article/pii/S0140197113001322

- https://www.researchgate.net/publication/233122934_The_Relationship_Between_Exposure_to_SexualMusic_Videos_and_Young_Adults'_Sexual_Attitudes

- https://www.tandfonline.com/doi/abs/10.1080/10720162.2012.660431#.Vwrx8qb2-Ud

Psychological Impact

- https://www.protectyoungminds.org/2018/07/17/5-ways-kids-brains-susceptible-porn/

- https://www.focusonthefamily.com/parenting/sexuality/kids-and-pornography/how-pornography-affects-a-teen-brain

- https://www.unicef-irc.org/article/1149-the-adolescent-brain-vulnerability-and-opportunity.html

- https://www.aacap.org/aacap/families_and_youth/facts_for_families/fff-guide/the-teen-brain-behavior-problem-solving-and-decision-making-095.aspx

- http://www.adlit.org/article/21409/

- https://www.ncbi.nlm.nih.gov/pmc/articles/PMC4274618/

- https://www.psychologytoday.com/us/blog/the-athletes-way/201312/why-is-the-teen-brain-so-vulnerable

- https://www.ncbi.nlm.nih.gov/pmc/articles/PMC3761219/

- https://www.secureteen.com/peer-pressure/study-links-peer-pressure-with-watching-porn/

- https://www.psycom.net/teen-suicide-risk-factors

- https://www.psychologytoday.com/us/blog/sex-lies-trauma/201107/effects-porn-adolescent-boys

- https://www.ncbi.nlm.nih.gov/pmc/articles/PMC5039517/

- https://www.psychologytoday.com/us/blog/experimentations/201707/pornography-and-broken-relationships

- https://en.wikipedia.org/wiki/Effects_of_pornography

- http://www.cam.ac.uk/research/news/brain-activity-in-sex-addiction-mirrors-that-of-drug-addiction

- https://www.yourbrainonporn.com/adolescent-brain-meets-highspeed-internet-porn

- https://www.mpib-berlin.mpg.de/en/media/2014/06/viewers-of-pornography-have-a-smaller-reward-system

Peer-to-Peer Impact

- https://pubmed.ncbi.nlm.nih.gov/25350847/

- https://www.verywellfamily.com/things-teens-do-not-know-about-sexting-but-should-460654

- https://drexel.edu/now/archive/2014/June/Sexting-Study/

- https://www.kqed.org/lowdown/28227/is-underage-sexting-a-crime-with-lesson-plan

- https://www.psychologytoday.com/us/blog/teen-angst/201207/the-dangers-teen-sexting

- https://www.ncbi.nlm.nih.gov/pmc/articles/PMC4477452/

- https://www.ncbi.nlm.nih.gov/pmc/articles/PMC3999298/

- https://www.criminaldefenselawyer.com/crime-penalties/juvenile/sexting.htm

Underage Pornography Consumption Impact Mitigation

- https://theconversation.com/it-may-be-awkward-but-we-need-to-talk-to-kids-about-porn-43066

- https://bmjopen.bmj.com/content/7/5/e014791

- https://issues.org/thornburgh/

- https://www.gov.uk/government/uploads/system/uploads/attachment_data/file/534965/20160705_AVConsultationResponseFINAL__2_.pdf

- https://namica.org/blog/negative-reinforcement-isnt-always-best-way-deal-challenging-behavior/

Cited Works

Campbell JK, Poage SM, Godley S, Rothman EF. 2022. Social Anxiety as a Consequence of Non-consensually Disseminated Sexually Explicit Media Victimization. J Interpers Violence. (May): 37(9–10):NP7268-NP7288. doi: 10.1177/0886260520967150. Epub 2020 Oct 27. PMID: 33107385.

Dutkiewicz E, Russo G, Lee S, Bentz, C. 2020. SignBase, a Collection of Geometric Signs on Mobile Objects in the Paleolithic. Sci Data. (October): 7(1):364. doi: 10.1038/s41597-020-00704-x. PMID: 33097734; PMCID: PMC7585433.

Fritz N, Malic V, Fu TC, Paul B, Zhou Y, Dodge B, Fortenberry JD, Herbenick D. 2022. Porn Sex versus Real Sex: Sexual Behaviors Reported by a U.S. Probability Survey Compared to Depictions of Sex in Mainstream internet-Based Male-Female Pornography. Arch Sex Behav. (February): 51(2):1187–1200. doi: 10.1007/s10508-021-02175-6. Epub 2022 Feb 14. PMID: 35165802; PMCID: PMC8853281.

Gola M, Wordecha M, Sescousse G, Lew-Starowicz M, Kossowski B, Wypych M, Makeig S, Potenza MN, Marchewka A. 2017. Can Pornography be Addictive? An fMRI Study of Men Seeking Treatment for Problematic Pornography Use. Neuropsychopharmacology. (September): 42(10):2021–31. doi: 10.1038/npp.2017.78. Epub 2017 Apr 14. PMID: 28409565; PMCID: PMC5561346.

Jacobs T, Geysemans B, Van Hal G, Glazemakers I, Fog-Poulsen K, Vermandel A, De Wachter S, De Win G. 2021. Associations Between Online Pornography Consumption and Sexual Dysfunction in Young Men: Multivariate Analysis Based on an International Web-Based Survey. JMIR Public Health Surveill. (October 21): 7(10):e32542. doi: 10.2196/32542. PMID: 34534092; PMCID: PMC8569536.

Kalampalikis A, Michala L. 2023. Cosmetic Labiaplasty on Minors: A Review of Current Trends and Evidence. Int J Impot Res. (May): 35(3):192–95. doi: 10.1038/s41443-021-00480-1. Epub 2021 Oct 18. PMID: 34663925; PMCID: PMC8522251.

Kamvar M, Baluja S. 2006. A Large Scale Study of Wireless Search Behaviors: Google Mobile Search. Proceedings of the SIGCHI Conference on Human Factors in Computing Systems. Association for Computer Machinery, New York, NY, USA, 701–09. https://doi.org/10.1145/1124772.1124877

Love T, Laier C, Brand M, Hatch L, Hajela R. 2015. Neuroscience of internet Pornography Addiction: A Review and Update. Behav Sci (Basel). (September): 5(3):388–433. doi: 10.3390/bs5030388. PMID: 26393658; PMCID: PMC4600144.

Park BY, Wilson G, Berger J, Christman M, Reina B, Bishop F, Klam WP, Doan AP. 2016. Is internet Pornography Causing Sexual Dysfunctions? A Review with Clinical Reports. Behav Sci (Basel). (September): 6(3):17. doi: 10.3390/bs6030017. Erratum in: Behav Sci (Basel). 2018 Jun 01;8(6): PMID: 27527226; PMCID: PMC5039517.

Rothman EF, Beckmeyer JJ, Herbenick D, Fu TC, Dodge B, Fortenberry JD. 2021. The Prevalence of Using Pornography for Information About How to Have Sex: Findings from a Nationally Representative Survey of U.S. Adolescents and Young Adults. Arch Sex Behav. (February): 50(2):629–46. doi: 10.1007/s10508-020-01877-7. Epub 2021 Jan 4. PMID: 33398696.

Rothman EF, Kaczmarsky C, Burke N, Jansen E, Baughman A. 2015. "Without Porn . . . I Wouldn't Know Half the Things I Know Now": A Qualitative Study of Pornography Use Among a Sample of Urban, Low-Income, Black and Hispanic Youth. J Sex Res. 52(7):736–46. doi: 10.1080/00224499.2014.960908. Epub 2014 Oct 28. PMID: 25350847; PMCID: PMC4412747.

Rothman EF, Paruk J, Espensen A, Temple JR, Adams K. 2017. A Qualitative Study of What US Parents Say and Do When Their Young Children See Pornography. Acad Pediatr. (November-December): 17(8):844–49. doi: 10.1016/j.acap.2017.04.014. Epub 2017 Apr 24. PMID: 284500

ABOUT THE AUTHOR
John Van Arnam

Over the past twenty-six years, John has been acutely aware of the all-but-invisible health challenge to young people occurring in our society. Internet pornography exposure has now manifested into the inescapable alteration of our young people's personalities through their early and continual exposure to it and the clear connection between this early exposure and depression, aggression, loneliness, sexting, grooming by adults, assault, and intimate partner violence.

As a graduate from Syracuse University with a degree in psychology, John headed to the West Coast and took a job as a salesperson selling search marketing advertising to internet businesses. It was there he first observed the porn industry's dominance of the internet, at almost 20 percent of all searches. He witnessed porn's seemingly unrestricted access to anyone. Collaboration with Yahoo!, Google, and Microsoft through 2010 furthered John's knowledge of the ongoing challenge to control inappropriate and undesirable content from an underage user's computer. John won awards for placing fraud filters and parental controls within the engines very early on in an effort to reduce underage exposure. John also was able to assist with placing a 1x1 pixel on pornographic websites in 2002 to guard against CSAM, which at the time was called "child pornography."

John recognized the slow infiltration of online pornography into the culture of our youth as nothing short of the hijacking of our young people's innocence, future relationships, and self-esteem. John realized that online pornography contributes to the development of risky behavior at ever younger ages and reduces the natural joy found in healthy human relationships.

It is from this knowledge and experience that John created The Third Talk, a fact-based, statistically accurate, and easily absorbable strategy to initiate pornography prevention conversations with your young people. A powerful advocate for healthy children with an unapologetic delivery, John provides straightforward phrases to start a lasting discussion within your family about youth exposure to online pornography. His work in schools, community events, PTAs, churches, and with individual families has helped him develop a unique and effective strategy for eliminating the harm caused to our children by this exposure.

Use the information below to connect with John and the rest of the team at The Third Talk.

TheThirdTalk.org

Info@TheThirdTalk.org

324 S. Wilmington Street
Raleigh, North Carolina 27601

Facebook.com/TheThirdTalk
Instagram.com/TheThirdTalk
TikTok.com/@TheThirdTalk
X.com/The_Third_Talk

Made in the USA
Columbia, SC
13 October 2024